BREAKTHROUGH THROUGH PRAYER

The Power of Prayer
Will Change Your Story

VOLUME 2

P-Z

Dr. Pat Akindude

Copyright © 2020 by Dr. Pat Akindude All rights reserved.

ISBN: 978-1-7354642-0-6

This book or any portion thereof may not be reproduced or used in any manner whatsoever without the express written permission of the publisher except for the use of brief quotations in a book review.

Printed in the United States of America

Publisher: The Master Communicator's Writing Services sharon@mcwritingservices.com Visit the authors website: https://drpata.com/

All Scriptures are taken from the KING JAMES VERSION (KJV): KING JAMES VERSION, public domain unless otherwise marked.

Scriptures marked AMP are taken from the AMPLIFIED BIBLE (AMP): Scripture taken from the AMPLIFIED® BIBLE, Copyright © 1954, 1958, 1962, 1964, 1965, 1987 by the Lockman Foundation Used by Permission. (www.Lockman.org)

Scriptures marked GW are taken from the GOD'S WORD (GW): Scripture taken from GOD'S WORD® copyright© 1995 by God's Word to the Nations. All rights reserved.

Scriptures marked NLT are taken from the HOLY BIBLE, NEW LIVING TRANSLATION (NLT): Scriptures taken from the HOLY BIBLE, NEW LIVING TRANSLATION, Copyright© 1996, 2004, 2007 by Tyndale House Foundation. Used by permission of Tyndale House Publishers, Inc., Carol Stream, Illinois 60188. All rights reserved. Used by permission.

Scriptures marked ISV are taken from the INTERNATIONAL STANDARD VERSION (ISV): Scripture taken from INTERNATIONAL STANDARD VERSION, copyright© 1996-2008 by the ISV Foundation. All rights reserved internationally.

Scriptures marked MKJV are taken from the MODERN KING JAMES VERSION (MKJV): Scripture taken from the Holy Bible, MODERN KING JAMES VERSION copyright© 1962 —1998 by Jay P. Green, Sr. Used by permission of the copyright holder.

Scriptures marked NIV are taken from the NEW INTERNATIONAL VERSION (NIV): Scripture taken from THE HOLY BIBLE, NEW INTERNATIONAL VERSION ®. Copyright© 1973, 1978, 1984, 2011 by Biblica, Inc.™. Used by permission of Zondervan.

Scriptures marked ESV are taken from the THE HOLY BIBLE, ENGLISH STANDARD VERSION (ESV): Scriptures taken from THE HOLY BIBLE, ENGLISH STANDARD VERSION ® Copyright© 2001 by Crossway, a publishing ministry of Good News Publishers. Used by permission.

ENDORSEMENTS FOR BREAKTHROUGH THROUGH PRAYER

Thank God for Dr. Pat Akindude's spiritual strength and the wisdom she projects in the tools in each chapter that are uplifting and encouraging. I have shared this book, *Breakthrough Through Prayer* with many family members and friends and they all agree that when reading this powerful book they have learned how to pray effectively. This book deserves a "5 Star" rating.

Ramona Pierce,
Higher Vision, President

It is an honor for me to endorse "Breakthrough Through Prayer" and the author, Dr. Pat Akindude. Prayer is a powerful weapon in the hands of believers, and Dr. Pat is an anointed, faith-filled, and skillful warrior. She has committed her life to prayer and intercession and to teaching others to pray effectively. Trust me when I tell you that she is not one who just writes and teaches on the subject - she prays and gets results. I am blessed to consider her a dear friend and personal prayer partner. She is among a short list of people I call on for prayer during the difficult seasons in my life, and I am confident that she proceeds boldly to the Throne of Grace on my behalf. Now, more than ever, we need skillful prayer warriors, and it is my prayer that "Breakthrough Through Prayer" will fan the flames that have been ignited in your spirit to pray bold, effective prayers. Allow the Holy Spirit inspired prayers and instructions in this book to equip and empower you to breakthrough to the next level in your prayer life and your faith journey.

Barbara Curtis
Bereavement Pastor, Lakewood Church
Author and Speaker

CONTENTS

Introduction	9
Passion For Seeking And Knowing God	10
Perseverance, The Key To Breakthrough	12
Power Of God Come Upon Us	14
Praying About The Joy Of The Lord	16
Prayer For An Exceptional Year	18
Prayer For Your Children	20
Prayer To Overcome Adultery In Your Marriage	23
Prayer To Overcome The Spirit Of Poverty	30
Prayer To Prosper	35
Prayer For Repentance And Forgiveness	39
Prayers To Swallow The Enemy's Attack	43
Praying The Perfect Will Of God	49
Reaching Your Dreams, Vision And Goals	52
See Your Dream And Envision It	57
Revoking Evil Decrees	62
Season Of Restoration	66
Singles Who Want To Be Married	68
Speaking Excellent Things	74
Supernatural Favor Of God	77
The Blessing Of Obeying God	79
The Blessings Of The Valley	81
The Faithfulness Of God	84

The Gift And Calling Of God	86
The God Of Signs And Wonders	88
The Lord Is My Shepherd	90
The Name Of The Lord Is A Strong Tower	92
The Power For Today	94
The Power In The Name Of Jesus	97
The Power Of Words	99
The Right Perspective	101
The Revelation Of God For Me	104
The Sacrifice Of Praise	106
The Wisdom Of God	108
The Vision Is For An Appointed Time	110
Touching Heaven And Changing The Earth	112
Unchangeable Changer	114
Waiting With Hope And Expectation	116
We Shall Carry Out Our Mission	118
What Is In The Name That Is Above Every Name?	120
What Do You Do When Life Seems Unfair?	139
Who God Is In My Life?	148
100 Scriptures To Deal With Issues Of Life	150
About The Author: Dr. Pat Akindude	181

INTRODUCTION

Prayer is the ammunition God has given to His children to help us navigate our way, deal with the issues of life, and come out victorious. Prayer invites the power of heaven to invade and interrupt the work of the devil in our lives and releases what we need to win. Prayer is the best way to hand over our battles to God, and He has never lost a battle, *"The LORD is a man of war: the LORD is his name."* (Exodus 15:3)

Prayer is fellowshipping with the Father; it builds our relationship, it opens our mind to truth, it gives our heart hope, our spirit strength. It is the desire of our heavenly Father to see us trust Him with our concerns through prayer. He encourages us to come to Him with them. The following scriptures confirm that God wants us to give Him our troubles:

PASSION FOR SEEKING AND KNOWING GOD

Matthew 5:6 *Blessed are those who hunger and thirst for righteousness, for they will be filled.*

Jeremiah 9:23-24 *"Thus says the Lord: "Let not the wise man glory in his wisdom, let not the mighty man glory in his might, nor let the rich man glory in his riches; But let him who glories glory in this, that he understands and knows Me, That I am the Lord, exercising lovingkindness, judgment, and righteousness in the earth. For in these I delight," says the Lord."*

Philippians 3:10 *"That I may know Him and the power of His resurrection, and the fellowship of His sufferings, being conformed to His death."*

Jehovah Shammah, The God Who is There, The Almighty, the only God that is wise, and all capable, The God who answers to no one, the One in Charge and in Control of Heaven and Earth. He is The Alpha and Omega, He is the First and the Last, The Beginning and The End. The King of Kings, and The Lord of Lords, The Ruler, The Commander in Chief.

> Lord, as we seek You, may we know You and the power of Your resurrection in a new way, and as we find You, let every limitation, setback, barrier, blockage on our path of progress be removed, in

the name of Jesus. Everything that concerns us will only respond from henceforth to the voice and Will of God for our lives. Our family, our spiritual lives, our relationships, our career, our finances, our contacts will only respond to the voice of God and no longer respond to the wicked ones, in the name of Jesus.

Let whatever we lay hands upon this season, bring much fruits, and succeed, failure will be far from us, in Jesus name. Father God, show us a side of You we have not seen before, help us come into a deeper level in You, may The LORD be nearer to us, throughout this year, in The name of Jesus. May this year be our year of significant grace.

The grace to be fulfilled, in all aspiration, to be blessed and be a blessing to our generation, in Jesus name. May this be your season of open doors, favor, peace, joy and divine breakthrough, in Jesus name. AMEN.

PERSEVERANCE, THE KEY TO BREAKTHROUGH

Romans 12:12 *"Rejoice in our confident hope. Be patient in trouble and keep on praying."*

Hebrews 10:36 *"For you have need of endurance, so that after you have done the will of God, you may receive the promise."*

Galatians 6:9 *"And let us not grow weary while doing good, for in due season we shall reap if we do not lose heart."*

Romans 5:3-4 *"And not only that, but we also glory in tribulations, knowing that tribulation produces perseverance, and perseverance, character, and character, hope."*

When we persevere, we don't have to fear, God is our Banner in battle, He is our Refuge from a storm, our Way Maker, our Hope of Glory, our Rock, our Defense in the day of trouble. He is our Hiding Place, our Savoir and our Shelter.

> Father God, as we persevere, may You grant us the outstanding results that will cause people to gather and celebrate our testimony. Let Your hand be upon us and enable us to overcome everything that is trying to overcome us. Every problem the enemy has thrown at us has an expiration date; they will all end by the power of God, we will hang in there

till our change comes. We shall persevere until we prevail. Let there be no more delay, no more hindrance, no more sabotage and no more obstacles to our moving forward. May the Lord rebuke every power and every spirit trying to hold us down, in Jesus name! We are blessed with all manner of blessings.

May God purify every trial we face and let it produce perseverance, godly character and hope! May our heart be genuine and filled with faith in The Lord, in the mighty name of Jesus! Father bring a quick end to the seasons of struggles, seasons of challenge and seasons of difficulties. Let our miracles manifest, in the name of Jesus. I thank God for taking us to a new level of glory, of anointing, of power and of blessing, in Jesus name! AMEN.

POWER OF GOD COME UPON US

2 Peter 1:3 *"His divine power has given us everything we need for life and godliness through our knowledge of him who called us by his own glory and goodness."*

2 Corinthians 12:9 *"But he said to me, 'My grace is sufficient for you, for my power is made perfect in weakness.' Therefore, I will boast all the more gladly about my weaknesses, so that Christ's power may rest on me."*

The power of God is what releases everything that God is into our lives and makes our lives work.

Lord You are the Owner of Creation and The Creator of all. The Giver of good gift. The Ruler in the affairs of men. The One who was, and is, and is to come, The Elohim, The Upholder of all things, The Sustainer of all things, The Everlasting Father.

> Lord, we thank You for a demonstration of Your power in our lives. May The Holy Spirit rest upon us, to defend and bless us, in the name of Jesus. May the mark of the blood of Jesus, the resurrection power of Jesus, be undeniable in all areas of our lives! LORD use us to manifest Your Power and authority on earth, in our world for Your glory! Let there be a revision, rearrangement, rerouting

of situation and circumstances in order to create a path to our desired spiritual miracles, in the name of Jesus.

LORD, release Your angels to enable and empower us in all our undertaking, that we may do great things, through Your power working in us, through us and for us, in Jesus name! May the Power of The Living God, bring an end to all the works of the devil. May all the good promises of God be fulfilled in our lives and we pray that we will be strong in The LORD and the Power of His Might, in Jesus name.

PRAYING ABOUT THE JOY OF THE LORD

James 1:2-3 (NLT) *"Dear brothers and sisters, when troubles of any kind come your way, consider it an opportunity for great joy. For you know that when your faith is tested, your endurance has a chance to grow."*

John 15:11 *"These things I have spoken to you, that My joy may remain in you, and that your joy may be full."*

Nehemiah 8:10 *"Do not sorrow, for the joy of the Lord is your strength."*

Jehovah Gmolah, The Lord Who Rewards, may You remember us. You are The Unchangeable changer, you are Unmovable mover, The Faithful God, You are Dependable, You are Constant and Consistently good. You are our joy and fulfillment. We bless You. We decree and confess that from now on, no matter what we going through, we will be strengthened by the joy of the Lord. We'll enjoy divine assistance from the Lord; therefore, we'll not worry, for the Lord will be with us. We will not be dismayed, for You our God, strengthen and help us, in the name of Jesus. Anyone wanting to oppose our success will never prevail. We shall divinely be assisted, as we call upon the name of The Lord.

May God strengthen us and be a refuge from the storm, our cloud by day and fire by night, may the Lord shield us from all evil, in the name of Jesus. We shall eat of Jesus, The Bread of Life, and have peace instead of a storm. Grace instead of disgrace. We shall have joy instead of sorrow, we shall have wealth instead of poverty, we shall have blessings instead of curses. Father grant us honor instead of dishonor, in the name of Jesus. Father God, use the very things the enemy had used to steal our joy, to bring us unstoppable joy. And because of Jesus, we'll have hope for a better tomorrow, our situation will not be hopeless, our future shall be secured, our joy shall be constant, our celebration shall not be cut off, in Jesus name! AMEN.

PRAYER FOR AN EXCEPTIONAL YEAR

Psalm 84:11 *"For the Lord God is a sun and shield; The Lord will give grace and glory; No good thing will He withhold From those who walk uprightly."*

Psalm 20:4 *"May he give you the desire of your heart and make all your plans succeed."*

Psalm 65:11 *"You crown the year with your goodness, and your paths drip with abundance."*

God is the Everlasting Father. He promises to wipe away our tears, to turn our shame to honor, to make our enemies our footstool, and if we cast our burden on Him, He will sustain us.

When man counts you out, He counts you in. When man says it is finished for you, God says, no, no, I just started with you. He will never leave you nor forsake you. If God be for you, who can be against you? No one!

> Father God, let us no longer encounter disappointments of the previous years. Starting today, we will start to experience exceptionally great days, may the Lord cause all our weeks to be outstanding and great. Throughout this year, we will experience extraordinarily wonderful months, in the

name of Jesus. May the Lord Himself, bless us with incredible and fantastic season for His name sake. Holy Spirit connect us to that which we have always wanted, good relationships, the joy, financial freedom, the incredible peace like a river, with total health and wholeness, in the name of Jesus.

May the Lord bless us with a deeper relationship with Him, a union and communion more meaningful than ever before, from now on, our lives will only respond to the perfect Will of God for us, from henceforth, in Jesus name. No work of the devil will come to pass in our lives, evil will be far from us and our loved ones, in Jesus mighty name. AMEN

PRAYER FOR YOUR CHILDREN

Isaiah 65:23-24 *"Their work will not be worthless anymore. They will not have children who are sure to face sudden terror. Instead, I will bless them. I will also bless their children after them. Even before they call out to me, I will answer them. While they are still speaking, I will hear them."*

Exodus 13:21 *"The presence of God will lighten the path of all my children, in Jesus Christ name."*

Isaiah 8:18 *"Here am I and the children whom the Lord has given me! We are for signs and wonders."*

Psalm 37:25 *"I have been young, and now am old; yet have I not seen the righteous forsaken, nor his seed begging bread."*

Father God, You are El Elyon, God Most-High. El-Elohe-Israel, The Personal God of Israel. You are our personal God, our Good Shepherd, our Redeemer, our Righteousness, our Father, our Maker, our Portion, our Keeper, our Teacher, our Advocate, our Mediator, You are our everything. Lord we pray that our work will not be worthless, our labor over our children will not be in vain. Our children will not be afraid of the terror by night, nor of the arrow *that* flies by day. Instead, The Lord will keep our children. Before we call on the Lord concerning them, He will answer, while we are still speaking, He will hear us, in Jesus name. Lord let all our children succeed in life and be well off, let them be an asset to the community, not a liability.

Father give our children wisdom, knowledge, and understanding, so that they will always make good decisions and choices. Our children will not be delayed in life; they will graduate on time, get good jobs, marry on time and have their own children on time. We pray they marry the right people, that they will not miss it in marriage. May they succeed in all areas of life. We pray all our children will know God, love and serve Him. May the Lord protect, defend and keep all of them. Evil will not know them, sickness will not visit them, in the name of Jesus. Our children will not die, we will not bury our children, in Jesus name. We pray that they will love and honor us and we will have favor with them, in our old age they will take care of us, in the name of Jesus.

In whatever age you are, your children will be mighty on the earth, because God will be with them. They shall never be forsaken, they will be a blessing in your life, all the days of their lives.

Lord thank You for Your protection and care over our families. May You give us the wisdom to lead and teach our children. Lord help us not to be anxious or overwhelmed. But enable us to release them to You, so that You will fully accomplish all that You desire, in them, through them and for them. May You fill our families with Your goodness and cover us with Your love. Amen!

PRAYER TO OVERCOME ADULTERY IN YOUR MARRIAGE

Father, in the name of Jesus, I thank You for being God, The All Powerful One. The Miracle Worker, The Everlasting Father, Maker of heaven and earth. The God who answers to no one, The Lord of Host, The One who says yes, and no one can say no. May You hear and use this prayer to bring an end to the work of the devil an to end adultery in my marriage.

Father God, I present to you this day my spouse, and I ask that you put the hedge of thorns on him/her, according to Hosea 2:6, to deliver him/her from the sin of adultery. Cause my spouse to no longer find pleasure in being unfaithful in this marriage. Father God, cause these ungodly desires to not be fulfilled. Let my spouse return to a covenant relationship first and foremost with You God and to this marriage. I pray for grace, patience and peace to guard my heart, as I wait on You Lord to bring this prayer to fulfillment.

Any sin in my life, my blood line or my spouse's blood line, that may have opened the door to adultery in my marriage, Lord forgive and short that door.

Father do not allow what trouble my parents or people in my family in their marriage to trouble my marriage.

Therefore, let every person, power and spirits working against this marriage be broken, scattered and be permanently destroyed.

Father God bring an end to all ungodly lust. Lord renew my spouse's mind and show him/her that this behavior leads to destruction and against Your will. Show him/her the consequences.

Proverbs 6:32 *"Whoever commits adultery with a woman lacks understanding; He who does so destroys his own soul."*

Proverbs 6:27-29 *"Can a man take fire to his bosom, and his clothes not be burned? Can one walk on hot coals, and his feet not be seared? So is he who goes in to his neighbor's wife; Whoever touches her shall not be innocent."*

1 Corinthians 6:18 *"Flee sexual immorality. Every sin that a man does is outside the body, but he who commits sexual immorality sins against his own body."* Give him dreams and visions to see that the end is of no good."

I pray that You will season my speech with grace, so that I will know what to say and when to say it.

I pray that you will cleanse my heart and root out any seed of bitterness. Give me grace to forgive. Put a guard over my mouth and show me how I can accommodate the reconciliation and restoration of this marriage.

Lord let any person interfering with this marriage become invalid, insignificant, powerless, useless and void. Let every seductive power working against this marriage be destroyed by the blood of Jesus.

Father God, let whoever is having an adulterous affair with my spouse not find peace or joy in it any longer. Let whatever brought them together be the very thing that separates and scatters them. Whatever united them, let the same thing divide them, in the name of Jesus.

If I have any incorrect response to what has happened, please reveal it to me. Forgive me God and prepare me for his/her return. Guide and keep my family with your Holy Spirit, in Jesus name, Amen

Let my spouse start to think about me favorably, let him/her talk about me favorably and respond to me and our children favorable. Lord establish closer loving relations with my children and me. Give me favor with them.

Father God, You said You hate divorce; therefore, let this marriage not end in divorce, in Jesus name.

Father, I stand on Your Word, Mark 10:9 *"What therefore God has joined together, let not man put asunder."*

I pray we will enjoy peace in our marriage, and God will preserve us. May You cover our nakedness and end the shame. We now by faith receive the anointing that makes marriage easier and enjoyable.

Let there be unrest, division and confusion in their mist, every time this person gets together with my spouse. Whoever is a tool in the hand of the enemy, to bring unrest in my marriage, may God rebuke you. May you never find rest or comfort in the arms or presence of my spouse.

Pray Lord, I thank You, that even now, right now, You are turning my spouse's heart away from this person, and turning our heart back to each other. I release the blood of Jesus to remove from my home all strangers, pornography, unfaithfulness, in my marriage, let the cross come between them, and the name of Jesus keep them apart, and the Word of God divide them, in the name of Jesus.

I delete the pain of shame, failure, disgrace rejection, physical emotional and financial abandonment, in my life, in Jesus name.

Genesis 2:24 *"Therefore shall a man leave his father and his mother, and shall cleave unto his wife: and they shall be one flesh."*

No more adultery, we are one flesh. We shall become one, friends, and lovers. Lord I bring this case to Your courtroom, judge between me and my spouse that is cheating and betraying my trust and give me justice, vindicate me and compensate me in the relationship.

Father God what you have given to me as joy, will not turn to sorrow because of adultery. Turn my spouse's heart from being unfaithful to becoming loyal, committed and loving. Turn my spouse's heart from being unfaithful to become selfless, truthful and changed. Let all lying and cover up be exposed and end.

Shortly, soon, and very soon, you will look at your marriage and shout for joy, for what God has done. Whatever is your prayer point today shall become your praise point and your testimony.

I bind and cast out all selfishness and self-centeredness, inconsideration, lying, and unfaithfulness in this marriage, in the name of Jesus.

I pray for you, that whatever is causing problems in the marriage, God will bring an end to it and start the healing process. Father give the spouse that is betrayed comfort assurance of Your love and care, heal their heart, and bless them, in the name of Jesus.

Father, because adultery hurts the whole family, if there are children involved, I pray You heal and comfort the entire family, let this wickedness not affect them negatively, but You be their example of faithfulness, love and selflessness, in Jesus name.

Lord let everyone of Satan's efforts, plan and strategy against this marriage fail completely. Heaven will favor you and earth will be good to you.

Jeremiah 22:29 *"O earth, earth hear ye the word of the Lord."*

Earth will yield its good to you. Let only Jesus be the only third person in this marriage, every other person or thing be gone.

When this is all over your marriage shall become the envy of many. As God shows up in your life, you will not have a better past.

Haggai 2:9 *"'The latter glory of this house will be greater than the former,' says the LORD of hosts, 'and in this place I will give peace,' declares the LORD of hosts."*

I pray for you all the days of your life, you will enjoy peace in your marriage, and God will preserve you, He will cover your nakedness.

Because you have been so greatly betrayed by the one that is supposed to love you and be faithful to you, God will reward you with His love. You will not lack anything called good... Even though this may be the most painful thing you may have had to go through, you will become better for it, your character will become more Christlike.

I pray God gives you the grace to forgive your spouse and the other person, and bless you with a beautiful loving marriage, better than it was before the adultery. Your marriage bed shall no longer be defiled, in Jesus name. The Lord that rewrites history and story will rewrite your history and change your story. This will not define you, but it will refine you. "Finally, be strong in the Lord and in his mighty power."

PRAYER TO OVERCOME THE SPIRIT OF POVERTY

God is our loving Father that is pleased to see His children prosper in all areas of life. He has made it clear all through the scriptures that He is our source and resource. He wants to meet all our needs, as we trust Him. We can go after our wants, and God will enable us if we want to prosper for the right reason, to be a blessing.

We are blessed, to be a blessing. Luke 6:38 *"Give, and it will be given to you: good measure, pressed down, shaken together, and running over will be put into your bosom. For with the same measure that you use, it will be measured back to you."* Where there is a need for the kingdom or to help the poor, God wants His children to be in position to support and meet those needs.

The Lord wants us to be lenders not borrowers. He does not want us to be in debt to anybody.

"The earth is the Lord's, and everything in it. The world and all its people belong to him." NLT (Psalm 24:1)

"Just as the rich rule the poor, so the borrower is servant to the lender." NLT (Proverbs 22:7)

Our responsibility as believers is to love and not be in debt to anybody.

Romans 13:8 *"Owe no one anything except to love one another, for he who loves another has fulfilled the law."*

Whatever resources God has given to us, He wants us to be faithful with it so He can trust us with more.

Luke 16:10 NLT *"If you are faithful in little things, you will be faithful in large ones. But if you are dishonest in little things, you won't be honest with greater responsibilities."*

It is important that we understand the principle of seed and harvest. If we are believing for financial increase, sowing is important, sow into the kingdom and into people, especially those in need (the poor)

Genesis 8:22 *"While the earth remains, Seedtime and harvest, cold and heat, summer and winter, day and night will never cease."*

A lady was talking to the Lord as they were taking offering in the church, that she said, she would like to give, but did not have any money to give. The Lord said, true, because she is wearing the offering she was supposed to give. Many people eat their seed and during harvest they have nothing to harvest because they have not sowed anything, or they have sowed little.

2 Corinthians 9:6 *"Remember this: he who sows sparingly will also reap sparingly. He who sows bountifully will also reap bountifully."*

One of the most important things a believer can do for their finances is to be a faithful and consistent tither.

Malachi 3:10 (NLT) *"Bring all the tithes into the storehouse so there will be enough food in my Temple." If you do, says the LORD of Heaven's Armies, I will open the windows of heaven for you. I will pour out a blessing so great you won't have enough room to take it in."* Try it! Put me to the test!

The reason God said in the bible, bring your tithe, and not it, is because you don't give what is not yours, to the owner, you bring it. God said the first 10% of all your earning belong to Him. A person that does not tithe is like a person stealing directly from the offering bowl when it is passed around. Some people think pastors stress on the tithe because they want it for their church. No, it is God's command, with great blessings promised, if you do it. I don't believe a person can know God, fear Him and Love Him, and not tithe. Obedient or disobedient in tithing reveals a lot about our heart.

Matthew 6:21 *"For where your treasure is, there your heart will be also."* If you invest in the things of God, there is a good chance your heart is also with Him.

True blessings come from God. Jeremiah 17:7-8 NLT *"But blessed are those who trust in the Lord and have made the Lord their hope and confidence. They are like trees planted along a riverbank, with roots that reach deep into the water. Such trees are not bothered by the heat or worried by long months of drought. Their leaves stay green, and they never stop producing fruit."*

When wealth comes through ungodly means, it's not enjoyable. It is only the blessings of God that you enjoy, and no evil is added.

Proverbs. 10:22 *"The blessing of the Lord makes one rich, And He adds no sorrow with it."*

Prayer changes things, may God use these prayers to change your financial story for good, in Jesus name.

Prayer Points:

- Let every altar of poverty, working against my prosperity burn to ashes. By the power of the Holy Ghost, let the altar of continuous prosperity be raised in my life, in the name of Jesus.

- Every stronghold of spiritual and mental poverty in my bloodline be broken and permanently destroyed in my life. I break and lose myself from every spirit of inherited and generational poverty. Abraham's blessings are mine.

- I reject every negative perspective that is allowing financial lack in my life. I command it to come to a quick end. I have the mind of Christ.

- Father God, I bless You for opening doors of opportunity in my life, open doors that no man can shut and shut doors that no man can open. I bind and cast out every word enforcing poverty in my life. Blood of Jesus erase every word working against my prosperity, spoken by others or me in, Jesus name.

- Father God, bring an end to all financial lack, financial dryness, financial barrenness and financial desert, in the name of Jesus.

- Lord, I thank You for inspired ideas to create wealth, I thank You for power to create wealth, divine ideas for creating wealth, in the name of Jesus.

- By the great power of God, I dismantle every opposition to my prosperity, in the name of Jesus.

- From today, my portion has changed from beggar and borrower to giver and lender. I am moving from low income, or no income, to having employees and paying them salary. I am moving from overdraft to having big good investments, in Jesus name.

- Almighty God, let Your glory and favor rest upon the work of my hand. Wherever my name shows up, Lord grant me favor with You and with man. Let whatever I touch prosper, in the name of Jesus.

- By the anointing of The Most-High, I call in financial resource from the North, South, West and East. I have provision for all my need, and overflow to help others.

- All my bills are paid, I am out of debt, and I shall live in financial freedom to leave an inheritance for my children's children.

- Every witchcraft spirit troubling my finances, may The Lord rebuke you. I come against you by the power of The Holy Ghost, in the name of Jesus.

- Blood of Jesus, wash away every mark of poverty in my life. I bear in my body the mark of The Lord Jesus Christ, therefore let no evil power of lack trouble me.

PRAYER TO PROSPER

Almighty God, You are The Owner of Heaven and Earth. The Creator of all things. Your name is Jehovah Jireh, our Great Provider. The One that can bring something out of nothing. You are The Great I Am. May You be all I will ever need!

"Let them shout for joy and be glad, Who favor my righteous cause; And let them say continually, 'Let the Lord be magnified, Who has pleasure in the prosperity of His servant.'" (Psalm 35:27)

If you give to God, He gives back thirty, sixty, and one hundred-fold (see Matthew 13:23). Regarding tithes, He said in the Old Testament, *"Prove Me now in this"* and see *"if I will not open for you the windows of heaven and pour out for you such blessing that there will not be room enough to receive it"* (Malachi 3:10).

So, we are looking at a measure of prosperity that exceeds what we could imagine! God is saying, "If you want My blessing, give to My work and to other people." If you want to succeed as a worker, a businessman, or in any field, give generously of yourself, your time, and your energy. If you are generous, openhanded, and openhearted, you will get back more. That is the law of reciprocity. You receive what you give. What you put out comes back, only in greater measure.

The Bible says, *"Give, and it will be given to you."* (Luke 6:38). If you give good service, you will get back good service. If you give an honest, intelligent day's work, you should receive a promotion and better pay. If you give kindness and mercy to people, you will get kindness and mercy back.

Asking is a principle in the education of acquiring wealth. Receiving is always a product of asking. It is your responsibility and privilege to ask God for financial blessing. Pray, asking the Lord to bless you with money yielding ideas, pray for wisdom; wisdom creates the path to prosperity.

> Almighty God, bless me with the type of wisdom that will promote me, grant me wisdom that will announce me, Father give me the wisdom that will open great doors of provision for me and my family. Father bless me with big financial blessings to be able to bless Your kingdom with big donations. Bless me to be able to sponsor missionaries, bless me to be a great blessing to the poor, Father God, bless me and make me a blessing everywhere I go, in the name of Jesus.

"Ask, and it shall be given you; seek, and ye shall find; knock, and it shall be opened unto you: For every one that asketh receiveth; and he that seeketh findeth; and to him that knocketh it shall be opened."
Matthew 7:7-8

> Today Lord I am asking for financial provision. By your great power, let me receive financial freedom. Lord end dryness and financial nakedness in my life, let the season of drought be over.

Father God today I seek divine opportunities and elevation, help me Lord to find them, for your name sake. Let Your blessings locate me like never before, in the name of Jesus. Father God, I knock at the door of Your resource, supply my need in a supernatural way. Father open to me the doors that have been closed to me, let every door of treasure be opened on their own accord, in the mighty name of Jesus. Lord, show me favor in my business, ministry, career, and let me be well compensated financially for the work I do, in the name of Jesus.

Throughout the year and for the rest of my life, there shall be no financial lack, there shall be no financial disgrace. Lord help me come out of all debt, in the mighty name of Jesus.

Psalm 34:5 *"Those who look to him are radiant; their faces are never covered with shame."*

Father God, You are the Radiant One, help me keep my eyes on You, that I may be like You and look like You: radiant. Because of You, my face will never be covered. We reject financial trouble, creditors will no longer be calling to harass us in the name of Jesus. From today we are delivered from debt, we shall owe no man anything, but to love them. Thank You Lord for financial abundance, thank You Father for financial freedom, Lord thank You for financial overflow, Father thank You for financial breakthrough and miracle, in the mighty name of Jesus.

Deuteronomy 8:18 *"And you shall remember the Lord your God, for it is He who gives you power to get wealth."*

Two things to know about Deuteronomy 8:18.

1. Remember the Lord, that He is your God, if you going to prosper, you must remember, that God is our Sources.

2. It is God, who give us the power, to create, without God, no one can create anything.

> All the days of my life, may I never forget who God is, that He alone is my provider, no other. Father grant me the power to be creative and fulfilled, power to be successful and prosperous. Beginning from this hour, the God of wealth and riches, is working in my life and finances. Let a new chapter of business opportunity open for me, a thriving ministry, an amazing career be offered to me. I command every spell and enchantment against my financial destiny to be forever destroyed, the devil shall no longer have power over my finances, the thief can no longer steal from me, and the killer shall not kill my financial blessings, in Jesus name. My financial blessing and financial breakthrough shall be unstoppable. No force in hell can stop what God is out to do in my finances this season, in Jesus mighty name.

PRAYER FOR REPENTANCE AND FORGIVENESS

Hiding sin will not allow a person to succeed: Proverbs 28:13 *"He who covers his sins will not prosper, but whoever confesses and forsakes them will have mercy."*

Repentance is the key to receiving forgiveness: Act 8:22 *"Repent therefore of this your wickedness, and pray God if perhaps the thought of your heart may be forgiven you."*

Acts 3:19 *"Repent therefore and be converted, that your sins may be blotted out, so that times of refreshing may come from the presence of the Lord."*

Our first step is to allow God to wash Satan's influence from our minds. This takes place through recognizing and acknowledging our sins and repenting of them. The Scriptures compare this transformation from Satan's way of thinking to coming back to life from the dead Ephesians 2:1-3 NLT *"Once you were dead because of your disobedience and your many sins. ² You used to live in sin, just like the rest of the world, obeying the devil—the commander of the powers in the unseen world.[a] He is the spirit at work in the hearts of those who refuse to obey God. ³ All of us used to live that way, following the passionate desires and inclinations of our sinful nature. By our very nature we were subject to God's anger, just like everyone else."*

Submit to God:

When we begin to truly repent and submit to God from the heart, we will begin to take His Word seriously and to obey His instruction and commands. Then His Word, the Bible, begins cleaning up our minds, washing away our evil thoughts, desires and motives. All who genuinely repent, who wholeheartedly surrender their will to God and are baptized may receive the Holy Spirit, who is placed by Jesus Christ into His people.

Put on the Whole Armor Of God:

But what can we do about the devil's attempts to influence us in the future? Here, too, God provides us with a defense: *"Finally, be strong in the Lord and in the strength of His power. Put on the whole armor of God, so that you may be able to stand against the wiles of the devil. For our struggle is not against enemies of blood and flesh, but against the rulers, against the authorities, against the cosmic powers of this present darkness, against the spiritual forces of evil in the heavenly places. Therefore take up the whole armor of God, so that you may be able to withstand on that evil day, and having done everything, to stand firm"* (Ephesians 6:10-13, New Revised Standard Version).

The apostle Paul then lists specific elements of the spiritual armor God makes available to us. He compares the defense of God's servants against Satan's influence to a *"belt of truth around your waist"* and a *"breastplate of righteousness"* (Ephesians 6:14). He describes their combat shoes as *"whatever will make you ready to proclaim the gospel of peace"* (Ephesians 6:15). Their shield is their faith in God and His Son, Jesus Christ, *"with which you will be able to quench all the flaming arrows of the evil one."* (Ephesians 6:16).

Their resolve is protected by *"the helmet of salvation"* (Ephesians 6:17), the assurance that in steadfastly serving and pleasing God they will receive eternal life.

Be Active in Daily Bible Study And Prayer:

Finally, Paul says, *"Pray in the Spirit at all times in every prayer and supplication. To that end keep alert and always persevere in supplication for all the saints."* (Ephesians 6:18) These are the essential keys for warding off Satan's efforts to regain control over us.

The more our character becomes like God's perfect nature, the less Satan will feel comfortable in our presence, and the more he will be inclined to flee from us.

Prayer Points:

Luke 11:4 *"And forgive us our sins, For we also forgive everyone who is indebted to us. And do not lead us into temptation, But deliver us from the evil one."*

> Almighty God, I am sorry for my sins, I repent, please forgive me for all my trespasses, in the name of Jesus.
>
> LORD, by Your great and awesome power, I receive enablement to forgive all those that have offended me, hurt me, betrayed me, lied on me, rejected me,

violated me, attacked me or disappointed me, in the name of Jesus.

Father God, lead us not into temptation, keep us from every temptation set for us, let us recognize temptation and flee from it, in the name of Jesus.

In Jesus name, we overcome evil and all its power. Whatever is call evil shall not be our portion. Amen.

PRAYERS TO SWALLOW THE ENEMY'S ATTACK

To be swallowed means to be consumed, to be overwhelmed, to be drowned or engulfed. As you pray these prayers, God will cause the enemy to fail and release everything that it has swallowed up in your life. Serpent-like spirit can represent familiar spirits, strongman, witches, demonic agents and more. Serpents are carnivorous, they capture and swallow their victims Jeremiah 51:34 NLT *"King Nebuchadnezzar[a] of Babylon has eaten and crushed us and drained us of strength. He has swallowed us like a great monster and filled his belly with our riches. He has thrown us out of our own country."*

Most snakes have specialized body structures that let them swallow things that are larger than their heads or necks.

Synonyms for swallow include deplete, exhaust, bury, engross, get down, withdraw, finish, engulf, inhume, eat up, entomb, absorb, immerse, up, sink, eat, consume, lay to rest, soak up, wipe out, polish off, steep, plunge, enter in, use up.

> Father God, do not permit the enemy to swallow the blessings of God in my life, my finances or my destiny. Because in the realm of the spirit, the enemy also tries to swallow people's lives, destiny and purpose. Rise up and pray for the Lord to swallow,

consume, devour, overwhelm, and bury my enemies and problems instead.

Exodus 15:11-12 *"Who is like unto thee, O LORD, among the gods? Who is like thee, glorious in holiness, fearful in praises, doing wonders? Thou stretchedst out thy right hand, the earth swallowed them."*

Psalm 56:2-3 NLT *"I am constantly hounded by those who slander me, and many are boldly attacking me. ³ But when I am afraid, I will put my trust in you."*

> Lord do not permit our enemies to daily swallow us up, they may be many that fight against us, may You defend us, keep us out of their traps, deliver us from their ploys and holes. Let the mouth of the swallower be closed and bound, in the name of Jesus. Let all poverty and lack in our lives be swallowed up, in the name of Jesus. Let all sickness and disease be swallowed up, in the name of Jesus. It is for freedom that Jesus came. Father grant us that freedom, for Your name sake.

God Also Swallows His Enemies

> Psalm 21:9 *"You shall make them as a fiery oven in the time of Your anger; The Lord shall swallow them up in His wrath, And the fire shall devour them."*
>
> Father God, let the enemy of our lives be made like a fiery oven in the time of Your anger. Father God,

You shall swallow them up in Your wrath and the fire shall devour them."

Psalm 56:9 *"When I cry out to You, then my enemies will turn back; this I know, because God is for me."*

Father God, You are my only helper, I am crying out to You. May You hear me; as You hear, may You respond and cause my enemies to turn back, let every pursuer of my life for evil start to back off and back out now, in the name of Jesus. Father because You are for me, defend me for Your name sake. Thank You for doing it.

Do not let the floodwaters engulf me or the depths swallow me up or the pit close its mouth over me. (Psalm 69:15 NIV)

LORD, you are the God that swallows Your enemies, let me escape, and my enemies fall into their own trap, in Jesus name.

You swallowed Pharaoh's army at the Red Sea, let that be the portion of my enemies that refuse to back of my life and let me go.

I refuse to be stagnant, Holy Spirit, connect me to Your miracles, signs and wonders, in the name of Jesus, in the name of Jesus, back off.

I recover every blessing of the day and night that the enemy stole from my family and I. No more losing, Father God, enable me to come into a season of recovery and restoration, in the name of Jesus.

You caused the earth to swallow the flood released by the dragon (Revelation 12:16).

Father God, let Your finger cast out every demon and powers troubling my life. (Luke 11:20)

Let all discontentment, dissatisfaction, discouragement and defeat be swallowed up, by the great power of God.

Let all assignments of hell against my purpose be swallowed up. I reject and forbid every curse and negative words spoken against my life be swallowed up, in the name of Jesus.

"They will vomit the wealth they swallowed. God won't let them keep it down." NLT (Job 20:15)

My destiny and purpose will not be swallowed up by the enemy.

Let all the rods of the enemy be swallowed by the rod of God, and the power of the wicked be brought to nothing, in the name of Jesus.

Let every generational stronghold in my bloodline be swallowed up, let their power be destroyed, in the name of Jesus.

Let every accusation, charge, allegation, claim and persecution against me, in the realm of the spirit and in the physical, be discharged and acquitted, by heaven's court, in the name of Jesus.

Almighty God, from today, let every spirit that is not of You in my life be swallowed up: Intimidation, fear, insecurity, anxiety, shame, rejection, worry, failure, frustration, delay, limitation, hindrance, procrastination, poverty and sickness be swallowed up, in the mighty name of Jesus.

"Don't let the current overpower me! Don't let the deep swallow me up! Don't let the pit devour me." NET(Psalm 69:15)

Father rebuke every python and constrictor that would attempt to squeeze and swallow the blessings of God in my life. Lord by Your great power I crush the head of every python like spirit working against my destiny, in the name of Jesus.

"Arise, LORD! Deliver me, my God! Strike all my enemies on the jaw; break the teeth of the wicked." NIV (Psalm 3:7)

Let anything that comes to eat up my flesh, fall and be consumed. (Psalm 27:2) I come against any wave of the enemy that would attempt to swallow me up. Let not the waves overwhelm me. (Psalm 93:3) Let not the floods overcome and drown me. You are the God that swallow's death in victory. Let all spirits of death and destruction be swallowed up. Let spirits of the deep, the pit, and the abyss, be swallowed up.

PRAYING THE PERFECT WILL OF GOD

Prayer is simply a way of lining up our desire with the perfect will of God for our lives. God cares about our decisions and choices. Deuteronomy 30:19 *"I call heaven and earth to record this day against you, that I have set before you life and death, blessing and cursing: therefore choose life, that both thou and thy seed may live."*

Psalm 48:14 *"For this God is our God for ever and ever: he will be our guide even unto death."* God is interested in our choices; He wants us to make good ones. He wants most importantly our choices to reflect His will and plans for us. Ephesians 5:17 *"Therefore do not be unwise, but understand what the will of the Lord is."*

Galatians 1:4 *"...who gave Himself for our sins, that He might deliver us from this present evil age, according to the will of our God and Father."*

Psalm 89:21 *"With whom My hand shall be established; Also My arm shall strengthen him."*

> The El Shaddai, The All Sufficient One, You are Worthy. The Lover of our soul, we Honor You. Our Strength in weakness, we appreciate You. Our embracer when rejected, we thank You. Our great hope in hopelessness, we trust You. Courage for the fearful, we depend on You. Wealth for the poor,

we look to You. Almighty God, may You establish Yourself through our lives, let Your hands be upon us. Let Your wisdom and grace be upon everything we do. Like Joseph, lift us up for Your purpose to be carried out. Like Deborah, let us be used to do the unusual as leaders. Like Mary, bless us to be surrendered, in the plans of the kingdom. Like Moses' mother Jochebed, who refused to let her son of purpose be killed in Egypt. Like Paul, we surrender to be used to touch lives for generations, to expand the kingdom. Father count us in to be part of Your mighty work on earth. As You used all the men and women in the bible, here we are sent us.

Give us strengths in all areas that the enemy has attacked us, help us be strong, in Jesus name. Let all that we do demonstrate Your glorious power and goodness. Let our works show Your wonder to our generation, and may our lives, display Your love. Let all who see us, see God and see Your glory, in the name of Jesus. Lord show Yourself strong, and let it be known that You are our God, in Jesus name. AMEN.

Father God, give me the grace to look to You and no other for all my needs. Let me never forget that You alone are my source and resource. My hope and faith are in You Lord. Let me fall in love with all that You desire for my life, in Jesus name. Lord help me to get it; where my parents missed it, let me not miss Your plans and purpose for me. I bless You for being God all by Yourself!

REACHING YOUR DREAMS, VISION AND GOALS

Here are some tools to turning your dreams, vision and goals into reality.

You discover your dreams through the dream giver, God, He gives it, and helps you birth it. He gives it life and significance. It is important to see things with the eyes of faith. Before you can ever accomplish anything meaningful in life, you have to see what God sees, so you can carry out what God can do in your life. Once you are able to see what God can do, then you can corporate with His plans for you. *Zechariah* said in Luke 1:18 *"How will I know this for certain?"* His mouth had to be short for him to corporate with heaven's plans for the earth through him. God did not want him speaking unbelief.

Do not allow your past disappointment hinder or stop you from believing, expecting and reaching…

Michelangelo once said: "The greater danger for most of us is not that our aim is too high and we miss it, but that it is too low and we reach it." God wants us to dream big.

There is greatness that lies within you.

Don't give into mediocre and settle for less than you are capable of; don't settle for less than all that God has for you.

We serve a great God, who wants to do exceedingly abundantly above all we ask or think.

The Lord gives your dream meaning; He is the one that establishes it. When you are operating in it, it is beautiful, it is fulfilling. That is why the Psalmist said, *"Let the beauty of the Lord our God be upon us, And establish the work of our hands for us; Yes, establish the work of our hands."* Psalm. 90:17

When you are operating in this place of purpose, it may not be trouble free, it may not be big now, but you have a sense of peace, freedom, and liberty. 2 Corinthians 3:17 *"Now the Lord is the Spirit; and where the Spirit of the Lord is, there is liberty."*

When you are operating in your dreams, it will be undeniable; it will cause you to be known, recognized. Luke 7:19 and 22 *"And John, calling two of his disciples to him, sent them to Jesus, saying, 'Are You the Coming One, or do we look for another?'"...*

V. 22 *"Jesus answered and said to them, 'Go and tell John the things you have seen and heard: that the blind see, the lame walk, the lepers are cleansed, the deaf hear, the dead are raised, the poor have the gospel preached to them.'"*

He was making life better for people. He gives people life and life more abundantly; he was stopping the work of the devil.

Jesus did not say I am the coming One. He said, My purpose speaks for Me. Let what I am doing speak for itself. He did not have to tell them; John saw the heaven open and God spoke that I was His beloved son. Jesus was functioning in what the Father has sent Him here to do. When people that don't really know you are questioning who you are, let who you are speak for itself; you do not have to try to tell them who you are. You are a child of God, with purpose and destiny; if they don't know you now, in due time they will come to know you, in Jesus name.

1 Peter 4:11 *"If anyone speaks, let him speak as the oracles of God. If anyone ministers, let him do it as with the ability which God supplies, that in all things God may be glorified through Jesus Christ, to whom belong the glory and the dominion forever and ever. Amen...*

When God was creating you, there is something He has in mind for you to do, that He has wired you with the unique gift talent, skill and ability to do them. These are things that nobody else it equipped to do. Even if somebody tries to copy what you do, it is not going be as you, no one can do what you do, like You do it.

Your ability to dream and imagine is a God-given ability that He has given to you in order to reach your maximum potential and become a Champion for Christ.

The gift that is going to showcase you, God has already put it in you.

A man's gift makes room for him, And brings him before great men. (Proverbs 18:16) Joseph's dream showcased him.

Exodus 31:2-4 *"See, I have called by name Bezalel the son of Uri, the son of Hur, of the tribe of Judah. 3 And I have filled him with the Spirit of God, in wisdom, in understanding, in knowledge, and in all manner of workmanship."*

Your calling, gifting, ability, anointing and skills is specifically for you, for a specific time and for a specific purpose.

Joseph's dream saved people; Daniels dream brought God glory. Daniel fulfilled that goal by refusing to compromise. *"The people that do know their God shall be strong, and do exploits"* (Daniel 11:32)

Your calling is for helping others, one way or the other. It is supposed to positively affect somebody. Even the pain could be somebody else's gain.

1 Peter 4:10 *"Each of you should use whatever gift you have received to serve others, as faithful stewards of God's grace in its various forms."*

The pain along the way to purpose is for somebody else to gain.

All The people God greatly used, their pain, made the kingdom better: from Noah to Abraham, to Moses, to David, to Hannah, to Paul, to Joseph.

You have preplanned appointments and opportunities that will leave a mark on this planet forever as long as God is in it all the way.

When people dream without God, they find it hollow and unsatisfying.

But when your dream is God's dream, it's irresistible, irrevocable, inevitable and unstoppable. Most times it is unpredictable; you have no idea God would do anything like that through you.

Jesus came to reconnected dreamer with the dream giver God. Jesus said that apart from Him, we can do nothing; all our dreams will be frustrated without Him.

He said He is the vine and we are the branches. Branches only grow and produce fruit when connected to the vine.

So, the power, energy, and creativity needed to fulfill your dreams vision and goals must flow from the Holy Spirit. And you will be like a green olive tree in the house of God. Psalm 52:8

SEE YOUR DREAM AND ENVISION IT:

Once you are able to define your dream, write it down, Habakkuk 2:2 says, *"Then the LORD answered me and said: "Write the vision and make it plain on tablets, that he may run who reads it."*

> God takes pleasure in our dreams. You are unique and uniquely important in His plan for humanity. You are not one in a million; you're one of a kind. True vision becomes a part of who we are.

When you get to heaven, God won't say, "Why weren't you more like Billy Graham, or Moses, or the apostle Paul or Debra?" He may very well say, "Why weren't you more like you, who I made you to be? You were fearfully and wonderfully made. Did you follow your dream to the end?"

Discovering Your Dream

A dream is of no use unless it's discovered, just as gold is of no use unless it's mined from the ground. Have you uncovered and defined your dreams, seen your vision and reached for your goal?

Let's begin, seek God for it...

Since Walt Disney opened on October 1, 1971 it is the most visited vacation resort in the world, with an attendance of over 52 million people yearly.

At the Grand Opening Ceremony, someone turned to Mrs. Walt Disney and said, "Isn't it a shame that your husband couldn't live to see this?" Her response was, "He did see it—that's why it's here."

We must see the possibilities beyond the obvious, before it can become a manifestation.

So, see the vision in your head, paint the picture and write it down, and get determined to carry it out with the help of God. A person that has a vision is able to dream the impossible dream and live a fulfilled life. Your vision is your mission, purpose, values, strategic intent and goals. Vision can never be taken away from you – unless you allow it.

> Lord help me not to let go of my vision. Vision makes life worth living; Lord thank You for a life that is worth living, in Jesus name.

> May God give you a vision to guide and direct you, receive step by step direction. May He reveal His will and His plan by vision. Let your eyes, hearts, minds, and vision be open to God's will. May the Lord give you the grace and enablement to become what He has created you to be, may He help you reach the goals He has for you, enable you to fulfill His mission. I pray Father God will bless you with

a strategy to succeed in all that you do in this season, in the name of Jesus.

God makes the vision for your life possible, but you make the vision real.

Do not allow others to cloud your vision with their view, with their limited perspective.

When David went to the battleground where Goliath was tormenting the children of Israel, David started inquiring about what would be given to the person who kills Goliath, and his elder brother, Eliab, rebuked him.

1 Samuel 17,28-29 "But when David's oldest brother, Eliab, heard David talking to the men, he was angry. "What are you doing around here anyway?" he demanded. "What about those few sheep you're supposed to be taking care of? I know about your pride and deceit. You just want to see the battle!"

"What have I done now?" David replied. "I was only asking a question!" He walked over to some others and asked them the same thing and received the same answer. Then David's question was reported to King Saul, and the king sent for him."

There are dream killers and dream builders. Avoid the dream killers. They can be jealous, unkind and plain hateful sometimes. But you must ignore their negative words and move forward. If David had allowed his brother Eliab's negative comment to stop him, he would have missed defeating Goliath and missed his destiny.

Refuse to let go of your dreams. Do not let go of your vision, hang on for your goals: *"Where there is no vision, the people perish."* (Proverbs 29:18).

Stir it up, step out, get passionate, become hungry to carry out your vision, it is never too late, you are never too old to fulfill your dreams.

> Lord, help me invest my life in ways that will reap eternal benefits. Help me make a positive difference on earth.

> Ask the Lord to help you dream big, to not be afraid to want more, to not limit yourself or the power of God working through you. I pray you invest in your gifts and talent to give your best to the world that needs what God has put in you, in Jesus name.

Your difficult seasons in life are not random; they are allowed by God to prepare you for your next season. They come to change and transform you, to shape you for purpose and to the image of Jesus.

Paul said Philippians 3:12, *"Not that I have already attained, or am already perfected; but I press on, that I may lay hold of that for which Christ Jesus has also laid hold of me."*

We are not there yet, but we keep on pressing, persevering, holding on, fighting sometime, but we do not give up.

Paul is saying, I keep on growing in that which Jesus died for me to be so at the end I was able to say. *"I have fought the good fight, I have finished the race, I have kept the faith."* (2 Timothy 4:7)

He was saying, I got the dream, I saw the vision, and I completed the goal.

Do not leave God out of the picture of your calling: *"Many are the plans in a person's heart, but it is the Lord's purpose that prevails."* Proverbs 19:21

"Unless the Lord builds a house they labor in vain who builds it."

Commit your works to the Lord, and your thoughts will be established. (Proverbs 16:3)

A fulfilled purpose is what will cause you to leave your mark, that you have passed through this earth, and are instrumental in allowing the will of God to be done on earth. That is how you make a difference for the glory of God.

If you keep God first, you will never find yourself in last place. Psalm 75:6 - 7 *"For promotion cometh neither from the east, nor from the west, nor from the south. But God is the judge: he putteth down one, and setteth up another."*

Experience God, and you will experience your purpose. Dared to dream big.

Don't stop reaching, learning and achieving and believing God for all that He has for you.

You are not what the negative people say about you. You are who God says you are.

REVOKING EVIL DECREES

Revoking: formally cancel, call off, stop, withdraw, terminate.

For those who are under the influence of curses, spells and evil covenants. There is power to revoke or reverse any evil spell cast on you by evil people, that has been made available to you, through the sacrifice of Christ when He was hanged on the cross.

God has given us that same power, the power decree. Proverbs 8:15 *"By me (wisdom) kings reign and princes decree justice."* In the book of Esther, Harman wrote an evil decree against the Jews. After fasting and praying, the Jews were given permission to offset the evil decree. Esther 8:8-11.

I reject all demonic pronouncement from every evil altar against my success.

Jesus has already purchased our freedom from the curse of the law and all its condemnations by offering Himself as a curse for us.

Colossians 2:14-15 *"Blotting out the handwriting of ordinances that was against us, which was contrary to us, and took it out of the way, nailing it to his cross; And having spoiled principalities and powers, he made a shew of them openly, triumphing over them in it."*

I reject all enemy's reinforcement or re-grouping concerning my life, in the name of Jesus, they must scatter onto desolation.

Let every collaboration that comes against be exposed and fail, in Jesus name.

Let every access Satan has into my life be close by the blood of Jesus.

Proverbs 13:22 *"A good man leaves an inheritance to his children's children, But the wealth of the sinner is stored up for the righteous."*

Father God, enable me to leave blessings for my descendants and not iniquity. Let the wealth of the wicked come to me. It is written; goodness and mercy shall follow you.

I retrieve by the blood of Jesus everything I have lost due to evil decrees against my life.

Let every evil imagination, desire and projections against my loved ones or me, fail woefully, in Jesus name.

In the authority that is in the name of Jesus, I speak to the four corners of the earth to release it's good to me. From the North, South, East and the West, let all my blessings be released and let them come unto me, in Jesus name.

I decree and declare all my stolen blessings are released now by fire. I receive them and are restored seven-fold, in Jesus name.

In the name of Jesus Christ of Nazareth, I bind the spirits of pride, self-exaltation, religious spirits, Anti-Christ, judgment, anxiety, insecurity, destruction, torment, oppression, depression, hopelessness, suicidal consideration, pain in the body, headaches, bondage in the mind, hopelessness, feelings of guilt, and self-judgment.

Almighty God, by Your great power today, I revoke all satanic ruling concerning my destiny, in the name of Jesus.

Prayers for revoking evil decrees have to be said aggressively and violently. You have to pray like spiritual soldiers who are determined to win the battle.

I command every curse of impossibility issued against me be destroyed by the blood of Jesus.

I forbid satanic agents from deflect my blessings, in the name of Jesus.

Let every demonic declaration concerning my life fail, in the name of Jesus.

I command every satanic judgment and decision against me be rendered null and void, in the name of Jesus.

Let every tongue contrary to my peace and joy be permanently silenced, in the name of Jesus.

Let every altar of witchcraft, familiar spirits and false religion be broken in this nation and nations all over the world, in Jesus name.

I break every curse of unfruitfulness placed upon my life, in the name of Jesus.

SEASON OF RESTORATION

Psalm 23:3 *"He restores my soul; He leads me in the paths of righteousness For His name's sake."*

2 Corinthians 13:11 (NIV) *"Finally, brothers and sisters, rejoice! Strive for full restoration, encourage one another, be of one mind, live in peace. And the God of love and peace will be with you."*

Psalm 51:12 *"Restore to me the joy of Your salvation, And uphold me by Your generous Spirit."*

> Lord You are The Great I Am, Who promises to wipe away our tears, fight our battles and give us victory. You are the Mighty Man in battle. Make our enemies our footstool. Our Strong Tower, let us find safety in You. Instead of your [former] shame you shall have a twofold recompense; instead of dishonor *and* reproach [your people] shall rejoice in their portion. Therefore, in their land they shall possess double [what they had forfeited]; everlasting joy shall be theirs. (Isaiah 61:7 AMPC)
>
> May God restore our soul in such a way that will make us an example. Wherever we go, people will see us and know that truly, God has restored us.

Lord let Your accessibility and ability be renewed and reinstated in us. Promote us, like only You can. Lord, may You elevate us professionally and personally. Let dryness and lack be far from us. May all our delayed and denied blessings be restored back a hundred-fold, in the name of Jesus.

As the Lord restores us, may He cause us to laugh again, to have the joy of His salvation where there has been sadness. May we start to experience gladness and peace, in the Holy name of Jesus. Any power working to destroy our lives, we call Holy Ghost fire to destroy their plans and devices. Let all the plans of the enemy against us fail woefully, in Jesus name. We shall recover all the grounds we lost to the enemy, all the hidden potentials and gifts stolen from us shall be restored a hundred-fold, in Jesus mighty name. AMEN

SINGLES WHO WANT TO BE MARRIED

Isaiah 34:16 *"Seek from the book of the LORD, and read: Not one of these will be missing; None will lack its mate. For His mouth has commanded, And His Spirit has gathered them."*

Genesis 2:18 *"And the Lord God said, 'It is not good that man should be alone; I will make him a helper comparable to him.'"*

Isaiah 54:5 *"For your Maker is your husband, The Lord of hosts is His name; And your Redeemer is the Holy One of Israel; He is called the God of the whole earth."*

Jehovah, The Unchangeable, Intimate God. Your desire is for me to have life and have it more abundantly; You are the God that will never forsake me, You will never leave me, You will never mislead me. You will never forget me, You will never overlook me, and will never hide from me when I seek You. You will be found and when I knock, You will open the door. You are Jehovah Shammah, the God that is there. I bless You for being my Great Personal God. Faithful God You are!

I decree and declare, I shall not lack my own mate; let my season of singlehood come to a quick end, let my season of loneliness expire, in the name of

Jesus. So, the promise of "none will lack his/her mate" is for me, based on the Word of God, no enemy shall be able to stop it from coming to pass in my life. All the promises of God are yea and amen in Him. 2 Corinthians 1:20 (all God's promises are for you).

Jesus said, *"Therefore I tell you, whatever you ask for in prayer, believe that you have received it, and it will be yours"* (Mark 11: 24). Lord I believe, grant me that one that will be fun and loving to be with, Lord help me not to be selfish but selfless, and be ready for a blessed marriage, in the name of Jesus.

"And the Lord God said, 'It is not good that the man should be alone; I will make him an help meet for him.'" (Genesis 2:18) I pray today that God will repackage my life to be married, and bring an end to being alone, in the name of Jesus. May the Lord give me a makeover, spiritually and physically, that I will be appealing to the right one, making me irresistible and desirable, in the name of Jesus.

May God repackage my life for good, and make me a special woman, an extraordinary one, a virtuous woman, a wife material, one that is seen as a wife, even before dating, one that stands out for good, in the name of Jesus.

In the name of Jesus, I capture every power behind any marital delay, limitation, shame, and marital failure, in the name of Jesus.

May the Holy Spirit of God grant me violent faith to create my marital miracle. An undeniable miracle that will cause my enemies to congratulate me, do it Lord for Your glory.

According to Gen 2:34 *"the bone of my bone and flesh of my flesh, shall locate me and become one with me."* Any person or power that says I will not wear my wedding gown and have my first dance with my spouse, I bind and cast them out, of my life, in Jesus name.

Jeremiah 1:12 *"He will hasten His words (concerning my marriage) to perform it."*

May the Lord not delay in giving me marital joy; let this be my season of marital celebration, in the name of Jesus.

The powers that cause people in my family not to marry or stay married, shall not stand in my life. Galatians 3:13, Psalm 107:2 – I am not bound by the covenants of ancestors, and that I am redeemed by the blood of Jesus.

In Jesus name, I arrest and bind the ancestral, monitoring spirits assigned to keep me lonely. I disarm them and destroy the weapons they have been using against me. I destroy their control and influence in me by the fire of God.

I pull down every family altar that serves as an entry point for demons to seclude me from marriage.

I am ready to be found by my own husband.

I pray for you that your husband will find you, he will locate you, no more evil power covering your beauty and glory, in the name of Jesus.

That which you have been chasing will start chasing you, what you have been praying for shall no longer be delayed. Whatever has been militating against your rising martially shall be consumed, in the name of Jesus.

Proverbs 19:14 says, *"House and riches are the inheritance of fathers and a prudent wife is from the Lord."*

I decree and declare that I am a prudent woman that will soon become a wife, in the name of Jesus. May I become the person that attracts the kind of person I desire. I am sensible, wise, and perceptive. I walk circumspectly, insightful, and I am a virtuous woman. One that will be an asset to the right man, not a liability, in the name of Jesus.

Let every evil covering and hiding me from the one be set ablaze by Holy Ghost fire, in the name of Jesus.

May the Lord remove every satanic garment that is covering my glory, may The Lord put a rich robe on me, no more fitly garment of hurt, rejection, bitterness, unforgiveness, insecurity, pain abandonment and loneliness, in the name of Jesus.

From now on, I am open for love, companionship, laughter and my own season of celebration and joy.

Jeremiah 15:15 *"Lord, you understand; remember me and care for me. Avenge me on my persecutors. You are longsuffering—do not take me away; think of how I suffer reproach for your sake."*

God will remember you today and change your story. The God who remembered Ruth and changed her story will do it for you. No more delay in marriage; it does not matter what statistics say, God can provide your own in the mist of scarcity. Psalm 37:19 NLT *"They will not be disgraced in hard times; even in famine they will have more than enough."*

You shall not experience marital disgrace in hard times, in famine, dryness, lack, or insufficiency; you will have your own, in the name of Jesus.

I thank You for that mate, that from the moment we connect it will fit, we would be right for each other. One that we would look forward to coming home to me as long as we both live.

I pray by the grace of God, soon and very soon, I will walk down the aisle with the one, handpicked by God just for me, without delay, hindrance, demonic sabotage or interfering, in the name of Jesus. Father God, I thank you that all Jezebel and witchcraft activities are now powerless in my life and relationship. Amen.

May the Lord God Almighty lead me by His Spirit to the best person He has for me. In the authority in the name of Jesus, let the right companion be released to me. There shall be no more demonic delay, hindrance or sabotage to my getting married.

When this man sees me, he will know, I am the one, he will not procrastinate, hold back or shy away, but will passionately pursue this relationship with a desire for marriage, so shall it be, in the mighty name of Jesus.

Lord, Your word said if I decree a thing it shall be established. I desire to be married, I was born to be married and stay married to a God-fearing man, who will love me unconditionally. One that is mature, responsible, and wants to lavish His love on me; one that will challenge me, encourage and inspire me to be all God has created me to be. A Faithful Man, in Jesus name. Amen!

SPEAKING EXCELLENT THINGS

Job 6: 24, 25 NLT *"Teach me, and I will keep quiet. Show me what I have done wrong. Honest words can be painful, but what do your criticisms amount to?"*

Deuteronomy 23:5 *"LORD thy God turned the curse into a blessing unto thee, because the LORD thy God loved thee."*

That is the Area James said if you can control it, you can control every other area of your life. James 3:2 (NLT) *"Indeed, we all make many mistakes. For if we could control our tongues, we would be perfect and could also control ourselves in every other way."* It is saying if you can control your words, you can control every area of your life.

Don't use your words to describe your situation, use your words to change your situation. If you going to have victory and see your prayers answer, you have to start using your mouth in the right way. The quality of your words will determine the quality of your life: Pr.18:20 (AMP) *"A man's stomach will be satisfied with the fruit of his mouth; He will be satisfied with the consequence of his words."* The result of his words will bring him satisfaction. Your spiritual maturity can be determine, by your words. You can take authority over your life and situations through your words. The trajectory of your life, can be decided by your words. If we want to be able to carry out God's call for our lives, this is one area., that must be dealt with.

Almighty God, You are Jehovah Eloheenu, the Lord Our God. You are All Sufficient: When we sin and repent, You are faithful to forgive us. When we fall, You pick us up. When we fail, You give us another chance. When we are lost, You find us, when we are broken, You mend us, when we are discouraged, You encourage us. When we stumble, You stabilize us like only You can. When we hurt, You will comfort us. That is the Good, Excellent God that You are.

Father God turn every curse spoken against us into blessings, in the name of Jesus. Lord, give us mighty miracles that will compel our enemies to stop their wickdness. Almighty God, by Your great power, we shall speak words that produce life and not death, Father God forgive us for every wrong word, and deliver us from the consequence of wrong words, in the name of Jesus.

Let all our words be seasoned with salt, may our words, heal, restore, and deliver us and others. Let every evil word used against us no longer prevail. From today, our words will be gracious, loving, kind, powerful and anointed.

May our word not fall to the ground; may the words we pray come to pass according to the will of God. Men will respond to our words positively. May God be pleased with our words and bless our words all the days of our lives, in the name of Jesus. May our word bring us our heart's desire, may it bring to pass the desires of God for us. Let the words we speak cause us to receive preferential treatment everywhere we go, in the name of Jesus! Let those who hate us come and celebrate our success, in the name of Jesus. Father God use our words to bring us the right mate, restore our marriage, transform our children, and bless our business and ministry! May our words promote and empower us and heal our bodies, in Jesus name. AMEN

SUPERNATURAL FAVOR OF GOD

Psalm 90:17 *"And let the beauty of the Lord our God be upon us, And establish the work of our hands for us; Yes, establish the work of our hands."*

Psalm 5:12 *"For You, O Lord, will bless the righteous; With favor You will surround him as with a shield."*

Ephesians 3:20 *"Now to Him who is able to do exceedingly abundantly above all that we ask or think, according to the power that works in us."*

"The Lord is my rock, my fortress, and my savior; my God is my rock, in whom I find protection. He is my shield, the power that saves me, and my place of safety." (Psalm 18:2 NLT)

God is light, He is love, He is peace, He is joy. He is Lord, He is Goodness, and kindness, He is merciful and gracious, He is Faithfulness and Gentleness. He is God, He is Holy and Righteous and He is Powerful. "He Who Keeps Israel, will neither Slumber nor Sleep. Our God is watching over us with singing and His favor is upon us."

> Father God, let all the marks of disfavor and spiritual evil tattoos on our lives which have been hindering us in receiving favor be erased by the blood

of Jesus. Let the blood of Jesus erase the marks of disappointment, discontentment and dishonor. Let marks of sorrow, hatred, poverty, ill luck, sickness, failures, trouble, and all evil ungodly marks be removed, in the name of Jesus. May the Lord, rebuke and cast away demons following us because of these marks, in Jesus name. The Word watches us; let angels of the Lord follow us with the blessings of the Lord. Let departed glory of our lives be restored, in the name of Jesus Christ. Let the Lord do exceedingly abundantly above all that we ask or think, according to the power that works in us.

May the Lord surround us with favor as with a shield. Despite how hopeless things might seem, the Lord will lift us up. May God elevate us, may God provide for us, may God open doors for us, in the name of Jesus. Because our lives` is in God's hands, the light of God will shine upon us, in Jesus name. Every time we pray for favor, whether we are looking for a job, or believing for a mate, may the favor of God answer. If we believing for a financial breakthrough, may the favor of God make it happen. If we believe for healing, may the favor of God heal us. If we believe for transformation in our children, in our families, in our marriage, may the favor of God bring them to pass. Favor can bring prosperity. For God, delights in the prosperity of His children. Receive that power in Jesus name! AMEN.

THE BLESSING OF OBEYING GOD

Isaiah 1:19 *"If you are willing and obedient, You shall eat the good of the land."*

Exodus 19:5 *"Now therefore, if you will indeed obey My voice and keep My covenant, then you shall be a special treasure to Me above all people; for all the earth is Mine."*

Jeremiah 26:13 *"Now therefore, amend your ways and your doings, and obey the voice of the Lord your God; then the Lord will relent concerning the doom that He has pronounced against you."*

Jehovah Jireh, The Lord My Provider, The Most-High God, The Almighty, The only God that is wise; every other god is a fool. The God who answers to no one, The One in Charge and in Control of Heaven and Earth, I worship You today! May You bless me with an obedient heart, so that I'll eat the good of the land. Father God, arise and defeat every ungodly spirit operating in my life and my environment. I pray to be delivered from every unrighteous life style and compromise, in the name of Jesus. Let the Holy Spirit cause truth to operate in me, through me, and for me. Holy Spirit of God, send forth Your Word and Your truth into my life, let it become easy to not sin, in the name of Jesus.

May the Holy Spirit, my counselor, give me wise counsel all the days of my life. I shall no longer be a slave to the enemy. I am empowered to overcome all weakness. Lord give me the grace to no longer be under bondage of sin. I receive anointing and faith to walk in obedience and freedom. Let the enemy flee from me forever.

I pray that the Lord will give me the grace to wait upon Him, so that He will bless me indeed. May God give me a hearing ear, a seeing eye and a heart willing to obey, in the name of Jesus. I pray today that the Word of God will build my faith, produce my miracle and release my testimony, in the mighty name of Jesus. It is well with all areas of my life. Amen.

THE BLESSINGS OF THE VALLEY

A valley is the low place where we sometimes find ourselves in. It is the place of trials and testing, where we have to patiently wait and trust God, believing Him to move, to come through, looking to Him for help and change.

Corinthians 4:17 New Living Translation *"For our present troubles are small and won't last very long. Yet they produce for us a glory that vastly outweighs them and will last forever!"*

Psalm 46:1 *"God is our refuge and strength, a very present help in trouble."*

Joshua 1:9 *"Have I not commanded you? Be strong and of good courage; do not be afraid, nor be dismayed, for the Lord your God is with you wherever you go."*

2 Peter 2:9 *"The Lord knows how to rescue the godly from trials..."* the system, strategy, unusual way to bring you out.

> Lord let this valley be a light, momentary affliction that is working for me, and it will produce eternal value. In this valley, Lord use the plot and devises of the enemy to promote me and take me to that place of purpose and destiny.

Zephaniah 2:7 *"LORD their God shall visit them, and turn away their captivity."*

God Almighty, who was and is and is to come, The Great and Magnificent God. The Rose of Sharon, The Lilies of The Valley, Father God visit me and bring me out of everything that has me bound, remove all captivities and set me free to be all You have called me to be, in the name of Jesus. May every witchcraft conspiracy to frustrate my life scatter, in the name of Jesus.

Curses of barrenness and emptiness working in my life break and backfire now, in the name of Jesus. Lord in this valley, help me learn to refocus on how to reposition myself in my thinking. Help me learn that if I want a husband, I have to reposition myself to be a wife. That if I ask You for business, I have to think like an entrepreneur. Father God, help me not to look at You through the eyes of my problem; instead, I will look at my problems through the eyes of my God.

Lord do not let this valley be my final destination, but part of my journey to purpose and greatness. Let it be a place that God comes and meets me, to comfort, assure and bring me out better. Lord let all my valley of pain, struggle, disappointment, lack, attack, all turn to valley of blessings, in the name of Jesus. God is able to level out my valleys, and make them straight.

Isaiah 40:4 *"Every valley shall be exalted And every mountain and hill brought low; The crooked places shall be made straight And the rough places smooth."*

Lord help me escape from principalities of failure, frustrations, poverty, substance abuse, alcohol, sexual perversions, anger, bitterness, evil thoughts, low self-esteem, envy, jealousy and unforgiveness. I cut them all off, in the name of Jesus! Lord, don't let my story end in the valley. In this season I will change position from sickness to health, lack to abundance, shame to honor, pain to comfort, rejection to acceptance, a victim to a victor, poverty to prosperity, godlessness to godliness, in Jesus name. Father take the worst of my past and turn it into the best of my future. With God, all things are possible. He can make the impossible possible. My impossibility, can become possible through God.

THE FAITHFULNESS OF GOD

Numbers 23:19 *"God is not a man, that He should lie, Nor a son of man, that He should repent. Has He said, and will He not do? Or has He spoken, and will He not make it good?"*

Lamentations 3:22, 23. *"It is of the LORD's mercies that we are not consumed, because his compassions fail not. 23. They are new every morning; great is thy faithfulness."*

> Lord You are my Solid Rock, The Rock of Ages, The Unmovable and Unchangeable Rock! The One that is Faithful and Dependable, The God Who is Able and Capable. The Righteous and Reliable Father. I thank You Lord for Your unfailing love that never ends, help me to receive that love every day, let me experience them every morning, let Your Faithfulness, abide with me and my family as long as we live, wherever we go, let Your Faithfulness show up, in a mighty way. May Your mercies begin afresh in our lives, we receive Your unending mercies, in the name of Jesus.
>
> Let this season be the start of our knowing the faithfulness of God. We shall no longer experience evil, but goodness and the blessings of God, in the name of Jesus. In all that we do, let the Holy Spirit enable

us to commit all circumstances to Him and stand in faith until God fulfills His promise in our lives, in Jesus name. May we be spiritually strengthened to be used by God to bring hope to the hopeless, in the name of Jesus. May our understanding of Christ, of His truth, of His death and His resurrection be deepened. Psalm 143:1 Hear my prayer, O LORD, give ear to my supplications: in thy faithfulness answer me, *and* in thy righteousness." May the Lord hear our prayer, may He give ear to our supplications, and in His faithfulness answer us, in the name of Jesus.

We shall hunger and thirst more for God's Word and truth, so that our faith, our understanding will increase more and more, in the name of Jesus. May the glory of God, radiate in all that we do and be blessed with all manner of blessings, in Jesus name.

THE GIFT AND CALLING OF GOD

Romans 11:29 NLT *"For God's gifts and his call can never be withdrawn."*

"Without repentance" means that God won't change His mind about what He has called you to do.

2 Timothy 1:6 *"Therefore I remind you to stir up the gift of God which is in you through the laying on of my hands."*

> Jehovah, You are God of all, The Elohim, my only Hope of Glory. The Way Maker, Light of the World. I bless Your Holy name. Father God, thank You that You created me for purpose and greatness. Let all the good gifts you have deposited in me start to manifest, make way for me, and bless my generation, in the name of Jesus. Holy Spirit lead and guide me with divine direction and ability to fulfill the calling of God. May the calling of God bring fulfillment, contentment and satisfaction into my life and lives of those I am sent to reach. May God grant me faith and firm hope, perfect love, profound humility, with wisdom and perception, to be effective, in the name of Jesus.

Lord in this season, help me stir up the gift and be impactful; grant me the resource and connection to establish and use the gift, for the glory of God. I shall walk with divine revelation, insight and discernment, in Jesus name. I pray the lavish gift of God upon my life will be useful for His glory. Father strengthen and sustain me to move forward in Your perfect will for my life. Let no enemy be able to stop what God has planned to do for me. May I wake up daily fulfilling my purpose and destiny. Let the blessing of God rest upon everything I touch. I shall encounter His blessings everywhere I go and receive the grace to be a world-changer, for His glory. I am anointed, appointed, enabled, and blessed beyond measures, in Jesus name. AMEN.

THE GOD OF SIGNS AND WONDERS

Isaiah 25:1 *"O Lord, You are my God. I will exalt You, I will praise Your name, For You have done wonderful things; Your counsels of old are faithfulness and truth."*

Psalm 86:10 *"For You are great and do wondrous deeds; You alone are God."*

> Lord, You are great, and yes, You do wondrous deeds. Let us experience Your wondrous deeds this year by Your great power and love, in the name of Jesus.

Isaiah 8:18 *"Behold, I and the children whom the LORD hath given me are for signs and for wonders in Israel from the LORD of hosts, which dwelleth in mount Zion."*

> Great God of the Universe, You Alone are God, Faithful and Powerful. You are The Miracle Worker. Maker of all things. I pray that the anointing of signs and wonders will fall upon me; let there be a manifestation of unusual great things coming my way. Anointing for unusual favor, uncommon promotion, supernatural breakthrough, and unstoppable joy, in the name of Jesus. Father, You are The God of signs and wonder, give me the faith to

believe You for my miracle. I receive faith to believe for a major breakthrough, it shall manifest, according to my faith, in the name of Jesus. May the God of wonders cause a sign to manifest for me that will show the whole world that the Lord is God.

Almighty God, give me a new song and dancing shoes. Lord take my natural and make it supernatural, in all areas. Let my ordinary become extraordinary. I pray the grace of God that brought me this far will also take me where God has prepared for me to thrive, in the name of Jesus. I pray in this season The LORD will give me the miracle that I need for my story to change and my joy to be full. Let the miraculous work of Jesus follow me all the days of my life. May, The LORD, grant me divine encounters, with signs and wonders following, in the name of Jesus. I thank You Father for it. AMEN.

THE LORD IS MY SHEPHERD

Psalm 23:1 *"The Lord is my shepherd; I shall not want. V5: You prepare a table before me in the presence of my enemies; You anoint my head with oil; My cup runs over."*

1 Chronicles 29:12. *"Both riches and honor come from You, And You reign over all. In Your hand is power and might; In Your hand it is to make great And to give strength to all."*

> Lord You are The Almighty, Great King of Glory, The I Am, that I Am. You Alone are Worthy of Praise Honor and Adoration. Father God, You are my Shepherd, and I will want for nothing. You have always been there for me, even when others were not. You did not leave me. THANK YOU! You are the God that riches and honor comes from, who reign over all, let my life, reflect who You are, let it reflect Your riches and honor, in the name of Jesus. Where I have been poor, destitute, and dishonored, let who You are replace that, in the name of Jesus. Lord Jesus keep and preserve me from all evil. In all that I go through, may You be with me and let none of life's experience cause me to stumble, for the presence of the Lord shall comfort me. Father reveal Yourself in a new way, let Your

presence grant me unprecedented favor and breakthrough, in the name of Jesus.

Lord Jesus, lead me to a wealthy place, with You. In the presence of my enemy, may You set a banquet before me. Father anoint my head with oil and cause favor, blessings, healing and deliverance to rest upon my life. Father God, put a mark of Heaven on me, and I will dwell in Your presence, forever and ever, in Jesus name. AMEN.

THE NAME OF THE LORD IS A STRONG TOWER

Proverbs 18:10 *"The name of the LORD is a strong tower: the righteous runs into it and is safe."*

Psalm 61:3 *"For You have been a refuge for me, A tower of strength against the enemy."*

Lord Your name is the name that is above all names. In Your name there is victory, healing, deliverance and power. At the mention of Your name every knee shall bow and every tongue shall confess that Jesus Christ is Lord. I pray that everything that God is and everything that His name represents will start to manifest in my life in a new way. Let His glory be evidenced in my entire undertaking. May God bless me and may His goodness be obvious in my life, may it be undeniable. May the victory and blessings in His name be mine. I pray that the name of the Lord will favor me in a new way, in an unusual way. Let there be provision for every need, protection for every battle, and elevation for my breakthrough. Let the name of the Lord heal me in all areas, physically, financially, spiritually and mentally. Let God show me all His goodness, in Jesus name. Let that which wants to hinder my blessings and greatness be smashed to pieces. May the name of the Lord expand my ability and capacity. Let the name of the Lord enable me to do better in all areas, in the name of Jesus.

Let the name of Jesus silence every wrong voice in my life, silence voices of sickness, pain and poverty, let it silence rejection and loneliness. Let the name of Jesus silence witchcrafts and demonic activities, may it silence every attack confronting my destiny, in the name of Jesus. Lord, you are my Hiding Place, hide me, keep my loved ones and me from harm and danger. Father keep us from every fiery dart of the enemy, in the name of Jesus. We will stand and overcome every plans of the devil. Today, as I call on the name of the Lord, He shall deliver me from every evil power and spirit, in the name of our Lord Jesus Christ. He will deliver my family from all attack; He will deliver us from failure, curses, and generational curses, in Jesus name. We are blessed with all manners of blessings, in Jesus name. Amen.

THE POWER FOR TODAY

Hebrews 1:3 (NLT) *"The Son radiates God's own glory and expresses the very character of God, and he sustains everything by the mighty power of his command. When he had cleansed us from our sins, he sat down in the place of honor at the right hand of the majestic God in heaven."*

Luke 5:15 (NLT) *"But despite Jesus' instructions, the report of his power spread even faster, and vast crowds came to hear him preach and to be healed of their diseases."*

Zechariah 4:6-7 *"Not by might nor by power, but by My Spirit, Says the Lord of hosts. Who are you, O great mountain? Before Zerubbabel you shall become a plain!"*

Jehovah Shalom, the Prince of Peace, my Light and my Salvation. My Power and Empowerment. My Defense Jehovah Nissi. The God Who is Able and Capable. I Honor and Adore You. I pray that Your Power will fall afresh on me today in all my undertaking. Give me the grace to be victorious and blessed in all that I do. Let this day hold good news and favor for me. Father help me overcome every work of the enemy. Grant me wisdom and knowledge in all that I do today. Father God, help me speak with grace and understanding. Let my decisions and actions bring my desired results.

May the heaven over my life be opened. Lord release Your Power and anointing on me. I am redeemed from every generational curse troubling me, in the name of Jesus. The yoke of hard labor without profit be destroyed by the fire of God. By the power of God, let the curse of barrenness and unfruitfulness be broken in my life. May the Lord create a need and a demand for my skills, talents, ministry, anointing, business, and for my services, in the name of Jesus. Every witchcraft attack at the gate of my breakthrough shall all perish, in Jesus name. I pray from today, every power preventing the perfect will of God from manifesting in my life shall receive failure, disappointment, and defeat, in Jesus name.

Let the power of God be in full force in my life, let it move me ahead of the game, to be first and not the last, the head and not the tail, to be successful and not a failure, to be whole and not broken, in Jesus name. I have faith and not fear. I know the truth and cannot be deceived; I am complete in Christ, blessed with spiritual blessings in heavenly places. Transformed by the renewing of my mind, I have the mind of Christ. I am full of wisdom and not ignorance, in the name of Jesus. Receive the power to get wealth and be blessed in all areas of life, in the name of Jesus. Amen. I pray you spirit of financial destruction be put to flight in the name of Jesus. I reject all financial destruction, I cancel all financial ruin and financial devastation; no more financial damage, in the name of Jesus.

From tonight, I recover all that the enemy has taken from me, no more destructions, but success, favor, breakthrough, blessings and restoration, in Jesus name.

THE POWER IN THE NAME OF JESUS

Again, and again the Scripture tells us that in Jesus' name incredible things happen. Demons are subject to us, in the name of Jesus (Luke 10:17). Signs and wonders happen through the name (Mark 16:17-18). Healing happens in His name (Acts 3:6, 3:16, 4:10). The only name that can save (Romans. 10:13). We are justified in His name. (1 Corinthians 6:11).

Everything we do and say is done in His name (Colossians 3:17). Jesus has invited, urged, and commanded us to pray in his name and has promised amazing results.

John 14:13-14 *"And whatever you ask in My name, that I will do, that the Father may be glorified in the Son. If you ask anything in My name, I will do it."*

> Lord Jesus, because of Your name, I don't have to fear, my Savoir and Shelter. You are my Banner in battle, my Refuge from a storm, my One and Only Way Maker, my Hope of Glory, my Rock, my Defense in the day of trouble, A very present help in trouble, my Hiding Place. My Light in darkness, my true Provider when in lack, my Healer. The only name that Saves. I worship and adore You. Lord, let there be a revision, rearrangement, rerouting of situation and circumstances in order to create a path to

my desired spiritual miracles, in the name of Jesus. I run into the name of the Lord that is a strong tower and find safety, in the name of Jesus

Let every Word of God spoken concerning me manifest gloriously; I shall accomplish purpose and prosper in life, in the name of Jesus. From this day, may I live in joy and peace. As I call on The name of Jesus, let it bring victory to my life, increase to my work; may the name of Jesus bring profitability to my business, may the name of Jesus bring promotion to my career and blessing to my relationships. For I am God's workmanship created in Christ Jesus.

I pray that the name of Jesus will provide protection in every area, miracle where it is needed, and solution for all situations. Father God, let me not be undiscovered, unused, unsung, uncelebrated, unfulfilled, and unfruitful, in the name of Jesus. I decree and declare this is my year of grace, humility and dependence on God. It shall be a year of abundance, in The name of Jesus. I shall recover all the grounds that have been lost to the enemy. There shall be a manifestation of God's glory in my finances and health. Now, I receive power to be fruitful and be enlarged, in all good areas, in The name of Jesus. Father may You bless me beyond my wildest imagination and expectations, for Your glory, in Jesus name. AMEN.

THE POWER OF WORDS

Jeremiah 23:29 *"Is not My word like a fire?" says the* L*ord*, *"And like a hammer that breaks the rock in pieces?"*

Psalm 107:20 *"He sent His word and healed them, And delivered them from their destructions."*

Lord Jesus, You are the Word, The Right Hand of God. You are Light in darkness, our Provider when in lack, our Healer when sick. You will not allow the sun to smite us by day, nor the moon by night. Your Word is the Sword of the Spirit. You are a Man of war.

May the fire in God's Word burn everything that has been troubling our lives, burn them all to ashes, in the name of Jesus. May Lord burn all our distress, they will distress us no more, burn our worries, they will worry us no more. Father God, let every evil alter that has spoken into our lives burn with the words spoken over us. We are cleaned with the blood of Jesus.

May the Lord send His word into our lives and heal us, let His word heal our spiritual walk and relationships. Lord it is Your word we waiting for, let it come and heal our finances, and all that concerns us, in the name of Jesus.

Let us become strengthened by the Word of God, in our mind, in our spirit and in our soul. From this day, may we speak boldly the Words of God that will transform our lives, in the name of Jesus. We pray our blessings will be rapid; from unexpected sources God will bring our blessings, in the name of Jesus. May the Lord give us an awesome tongue and make our voice the voice of deliverance, healing, power, solution, and life, in the name of Jesus.

Whatever the enemy have been doing in the past that worked against us shall no longer work from henceforth. Every attempt of the wicked to destroy us shall backfire, in the name of Jesus. Every power uprooting good things in our lives, in our family, shall be consumed by the fire of God, in the name of Jesus. Every power blocking and limiting our success and delaying it, shall all be pulled down and cast out of our lives, in the name of Jesus. May the Lord repair all the damage done to us as a result of wrong use of our tongue and people's tongue, in Jesus name. AMEN.

THE RIGHT PERSPECTIVE

Perspective is not what we see, but the way we see it. Everything we do for God, is based upon our concept of God, based on our impression; it is based on our belief of God. Perspective is your interpretation of life, it is your own viewpoint, how you choose to represent things to yourself.

We become wise by studying and applying God's Word. It is the ability to see life from God's viewpoint and then to know the best course of action to take.

> Father help me to have your perspective, to see the way you see, to love the way you love; Lord this year give me the mind of Christ. When Goliath came against the Israelites, the soldiers all thought, "He's so big we can never kill him." David looked at the same giant and thought, "He's so big I can't miss." Almighty God give me Your clear and right perception. Human perspective is limited; God's is unlimited. Today I receive deliverance in my spirit soul and body. Let there be no more failure due to wrong perspective. Let favor replace failure.
>
> From now on I shall assess my situation with the faith that will produce my miracle. Moses had a human perspective: I can't speak, don't want to

cause any embarrassment for others and myself. He focused on his weakness, his speech, instead of focusing on the one who made His mouth. Lord help me see my problem from God's eyes. When God asks us to do something, He will help us to get the job done. He is able to provide the word, people, resources, strength, skills, and abilities, where needed.

Father whatever I need for the mission, may You give it to me, let there be nothing to hinder my purpose. Let that which wants to hinder my blessing and greatness be smashed to pieces. May the Holy Spirit expand my capacity. Lord be my Hiding Place, may You keep me safe from harm, and danger, and from every fiery dart of the enemy. Father God, enable me to stand against the wiles of the devil. In the desert temptation, Jesus was told by Satan that He could achieve greatness without the cross. Matthew 4:9 *"And saith unto him, All these things will I give thee, if thou wilt fall down and worship me."* I refuse to be deceived by the words of the enemy, to believe I don't need God, I refuse to listen to the lies of the devil, in Jesus' name.

Lord, I thank You for the right perspective, to see like You see and view things like You do.

Father change my limited outlook on Your abilities and power. Father, in Jesus name, let the anointing for a Godly viewpoint fall upon my life, in Jesus name.

THE REVELATION OF GOD FOR ME

Ephesians 1:9 (AMP) *"He made known to us the mystery of His will according to His good pleasure, which He purposed in Christ."*

Daniel 2:22 *"He reveals deep and secret things; He knows what is in the darkness, And light dwells with Him."*

1 Corinthians 2:9-10 But as it is written: *"Eye has not seen, nor ear heard, Nor have entered into the heart of man The things which God has prepared for those who love Him."*

But God has revealed *them* to us through His Spirit. For the Spirit searches all things, yes, the deep things of God.

> Lord You are The God Who Knows All Things, Controls All Things and answers to no one. You are Sight to the blind, Peace to the troubled, Strength to the weak, Present for the abandoned, wealth to the poor, health to the sick, husband single and widow and Father to the fatherless. Thank You for being all I will ever need. LORD reveal secrets that I need to know for my journey in life. Show me what is behind the issues going in my life, environment, and the world. Grant revelations of things to come and what to do, in the name of Jesus.

"You shall not be ashamed in evil times, in the days of famine, you shall be satisfied." according to Psalm 37:19. Lord, may You deliver me from mistake that will bring shame and evil time, bless me with the ability to know Your truth, in Jesus name. Let me not be ignorant of the devises of the wicked. Father may You always show me what to do, how to do it, where to do it, and who to do it with. Let me not move ahead of You in anything I do, but to look to You for guidance, in Jesus name.

Father God let me not be knocked down in any area of life. May You strengthen me spiritually, physical, relationally and financially, in the name of Jesus. May, the LORD, deliver me from all spirit of confusion, delusion, mix-up and lack of insight, in the name of Jesus. May the LORD lay His hands upon me, and make me whole, in all areas, in Jesus name. AMEN.

THE SACRIFICE OF PRAISE

Praise invites God's presence. He dwells close to us when we praise Him. He lives there. He looks for it. Our spirits are refreshed and renewed in His presence.

We're strengthened by His peace and rejuvenated by His joy. Through a heart of praise, we realize that God doesn't just change our situations and work through our problems; He changes our hearts and gives us His prospective.

Ephesians 1:3 *"Blessed be the God and Father of our Lord Jesus Christ, who has blessed us with all spiritual blessings in heavenly places in Christ."*

Psalm 22:3 *"He inhabits the praises of His people."*

Psalm 100:4 *"Enter his gates with thanksgiving, and his courts with praise! Give thanks to him; bless his name!"*

> Almighty God, The Most-High, The Great I Am, I give You Glory and Honor. You are Holy, Holy, Holy God. I Exalt You, I worship and Adore You. Receive all the Glory, Respect and Admiration. Let my heart desires always be to delight You Lord with my praise, and as I am praising You, may Your goodness and mercy rest upon my life. May the

Lord Himself respond to me and bless me in the area that I need blessing. Father, may You choose me in this generation to show forth Your praise, expressing to all how You have called me out of darkness and filled my life with divine light, glory and blessings. I pray that Heaven will open up to me divinely to intervene on my behalf, and as I magnify God, my troubles will diminish, my pain will be painless and my enemies will become ineffective, in Jesus name. I decree that my blessing will be magnified, my joy will increase and the Holy Spirit will be exulted in my life, in Jesus name.

Ungrateful hearts will not interfere with my inheritance. I will be the one that came back to say thank You to the Lord with my praise. I will worship no other but God, and God alone. He alone will be God in all areas of my life. Evil tactics and schemes of the enemy shall no longer distract me, in the name of Jesus. May the Lord bless me, may I always live under an open heaven, and may my praise and worship cause God to permanently display His glory and goodness in all areas of my life, in Jesus's name. Amen!

THE WISDOM OF GOD

In James 1:5 we find this wonderful promise for God, as He says: *"But if any of you lacks wisdom, let him ask of God, who gives to all liberally and with no reproach, and it shall be given to him."*

James 3:17 *"But the wisdom that is from above is first pure, then peaceable, gentle, willing to yield, full of mercy and good fruits, without partiality and without hypocrisy."*

Isaiah 11:2 *"The Spirit of the Lord shall rest upon Him, The Spirit of wisdom and understanding, The Spirit of counsel and might, The Spirit of knowledge and of the fear of the Lord."*

Father, You are the All-Knowing God, The Wisest God, every other god is a fool, ignorant, and weak. You Alone Are Capable and Powerful, yet Kind and Merciful. You are Highly Lifted Up, there is no one like You, the Pillar of our lives Adonai, Lord and Master of All. I pray from henceforth, The Spirit of the Lord shall rest upon me, I receive the Spirit of wisdom and understanding, The Spirit of counsel and might, The Spirit of knowledge and of the fear of the Lord. Amen! The Holy Spirit shall direct me, my decisions will be Spirit led and instructed, in the name of Jesus. May the Lord grant me insight and I shall operate in a higher and deeper dimension of wisdom and understanding, in the name of Jesus. May the Lord grant me sound revelation, peculiarity and uniqueness through His Spirit, may He show me understanding of my calling and mission in life, in the name of Jesus.

I pray for the fear and the love of God to be rooted in me. Father enable and empower me to always make the right decisions because of Your wisdom that rests upon me. May my purpose be made clear and the manifestation of God's Hand be on it and rest upon my life, in the name of Jesus. I pray the wisdom of God, operating through me, will cause me to standout for good, like Daniel stood out as an excellent man. That spirit of excellence will rest upon me, from this day and for the rest of my life, God alone get all the glory, in Jesus's name. AMEN.

THE VISION IS FOR AN APPOINTED TIME

God wants us to have a greater vision of who He is and of His great plans for us. Satan wants to distract us with lies and fear. The enemy wants us to compromise and settle for less. But if we would keep our eyes on God, He will do great and amazing things in our lives at the right time.

Proverbs 29:18 (AMP) *"Where there is no vision [no revelation of God and His word], the people are unrestrained; But happy and blessed is he who keeps the law of God."*

Habakkuk 2:2-3 *"Then the Lord answered me and said: "Write the vision And make it plain on tablets, That he may run who reads it. For the vision is yet for an appointed time; But at the end it will speak, and it will not lie. Though it tarries, wait for it; because it will surely come, It will not tarry."*

Jeremiah 29:11 *"For I know the thoughts that I think toward you, says the Lord, thoughts of peace and not of evil, to give you a future and a hope."*

The Lord is the Master Planner and Executor. He is the Strong Tower, my Banner, my Buckler, my All in All, the Glory and the Lifter of our head. When man counts me out, He counts me in. When man says it is finished for me, God says, He is just started with me. He will never betray me or forsake me. If God be for me, I know nothing and nobody, can be against me.

Starting from this day, the visions of God for my life shall be visible and they shall manifest. My blessing will be rapid. My vision will not delay. My expectation will not be hindered. God's thoughts toward me shall happen, His thoughts of peace and not of evil, to give me a future and hope, shall be so, in Jesus's name. I bind and break all witchcraft curses, spells, hex, evil covenants and powers of darkness; let them be cast out of my life. I am covered in the blood of Jesus. We command evil and demonic forces to back off and back out of our lives. We disable, disallow and disarm every assignment of the enemy against us, in Jesus's name.

Father God, give me vision to write and let my divine helpers run with it. May the Lord withdraw my family and me, from all satanic regulation, rules, decrees and governments, in the name of Jesus. Let there be unstoppable advancement, promotion, success in my life. May I fulfill my purpose and my destiny. By the grace of God, may He grant me great victory, in Jesus's name. Amen.

TOUCHING HEAVEN AND CHANGING THE EARTH

Christ has done a mighty work of salvation for us, that we may go and tell others about His love and goodness. He saved us to lead others out of darkness into His marvelous Light.

Matthew 28:19 *"Therefore go and make disciples of all nations, baptizing them in the name of the Father and of the Son and of the Holy Spirit."*

Ephesians 2:6-7 *"And raised us up together, and made us sit together in the heavenly places in Christ Jesus, that in the ages to come He might show the exceeding riches of His grace in His kindness toward us in Christ Jesus."*

God's desire is for us to have life and have it more abundantly; He will never lie to us, never leave us, never mislead us, never forget us, never overlook us, and never and never hide from us. When we seek Him, He will be found, when we knock, He opens the door.

May the Lord God Almighty grant me visitation that will change my story. May His Presence locate me and bring transformation. May the Lord grant me divine touch that will enable me to touch other lives for His glory. May He bless me with His divine blessing. May I be empowered to empower others, in the mighty name of Jesus. Let my test, become testimonies that will help others dealing with the same issues.

I pray as the Lord picks me to represent Him on earth, I will not lack any good thing. Throughout this season, may my life reflect God's glory and may He be merciful unto me. In every area of my life, let it be known that God is my God, and He is for me, and that He is greater than anything that can come against me. I pray this day the Lord will grant me an encounter with the third Heaven that will change every situation of my life on earth, for God's glory. I will be used in impacting humanity and magnifying God, in Jesus mighty name. AMEN.

UNCHANGEABLE CHANGER

God is able to supernaturally change any situation, without He Himself changing. He remains the same, but He does what He wants, when He wants, and how He wants it. He can do anything for anybody. No matter what it looks like, God is able to change it.

Malachi 3:6 *"For I, the LORD, do not change; therefore you, O sons of Jacob, are not consumed."*

Number 23:19 *"God is not a man, that He should lie, Nor a son of man, that He should repent; Has He said, and will He not do it? Or has He spoken, and will He not make it good?"*

Hebrews 13:8 *"Jesus Christ is the same yesterday and today and forever."*

> Jehovah, Unchangeable, Intimate God. He is the Unchangeable changer, He is the Unmovable mover, He is Faithful, He is Dependable, He is Constant and Consistent. "He Who Keeps Israel, will neither Slumber nor Sleep." He is the maker of heaven and earth. He is the High and Lofty One, the Pillar of our lives, the Lord of Host, the Lion of Judah, the Glory and the Lifter of our head. Father God, You are our Cornerstone. May You grant us

the ability to hear You clearly, and follow Your instruction for divine inspired ideas. Let every unchangeable painful situation in our lives meet with the God of possibilities. Everything that has been impossible become possible, by the 'Unchangeable Changer.' I pray He gives me a testimony that is undeniable, in the name of Jesus. I pray every unsuccessful project of my life shall change by the 'Unchangeable Changer.' May God visit me with His Power and grant me divine accomplishment, success and blessings, in the name of Jesus. May the favor of God single me out for divine help and promotion. Anointing of sudden change come upon my life and let it change for the better.

May God give me testimony that will change my level of acceleration and promotion; may He give me overflowing blessings, in the name of Jesus. May every satanic program from the pit of hell against me and against my success be consumed by the fire of the Holy Ghost. May sickness and disease run from me, may poverty and shame be far from me, may loneliness and depression not know me, and may my life change other people's lives for the better, in Jesus's mighty name. AMEN!

WAITING WITH HOPE AND EXPECTATION

Proverbs 23:18 *"For surely there is an end; and thine expectation shall not be cut off."*

Psalm 62:5 *"My soul, wait thou only upon God; for my expectation [is] from him."*

2 Corinthians 9:8 *"And God [is] able to make all grace abound toward you; that ye, always having all sufficiency in all [things], may abound to every good work."*

The Lord is the Lover of our soul, He is Strength to the weak, He is grace to the disgraced, hope for the hopeless, He rules in the affairs of men. He is the One who was, and is, and is to come. The Elohim. The Creator of all things, The Upholder of all things. The Sustainer of all things, Everlasting Father. He is Jehovah Shammah, God is there.

Isaiah 40:31 *"But those who wait on the Lord Shall renew their strength; They shall mount up with wings like eagles, They shall run and not be weary, They shall walk and not faint."*

> Lord as I pray to seek You, give me the grace to wait on You, trusting that You will perfect all that concerns me. Lord let my expectation not be cut off. Speak blessings over me, that I will find my strength in God as I strive for patience through all

the circumstances around me; as I seek God, may His strength be with me. Even when I cannot feel His presence, His sovereignty shall be over my life and situation. May God bless me, as I live a life worthy of the calling.

I declare and prophesy that in this season God will make all grace abound, and I shall have sufficiency in all things. He will confuse and paralyze all enemies. May victory and liberty be my portion. Let there be no more spiritual darkness and backwardness, in the name of Jesus. I pray every obstacle will be removed. Obstacle to my breakthroughs shall be crushed like the finest of dust. Father God, let everything that has been difficult in the past become easy and doable from now on. Father deliver me from those who hate me, cause all their plans to backfire. Father close the chapter of sorrow and open a new chapter of joy and peace in the name of Jesus. Lord close every chapter of failure and open a chapter of success and blessings. When I am weak and weary, Lord please renew my strength, empower and enable me, not to give up or quit till my breakthrough, break forth, in the name of Jesus.

I pray this season shall be my due season and my strategic season, a fulfilling season, a season of manifestation of purpose and destiny, greatness, and success. For surely there is future hope, and your expectation shall not be cut off, according to Proverbs 23:18, in Jesus name! AMEN.

WE SHALL CARRY OUT OUR MISSION

Ephesians 2:10 *"For we are His workmanship, created in Christ Jesus for good works, which God prepared beforehand that we should walk in them."*

Proverbs 16:3 *"Commit your works to the Lord, And your thoughts will be established."*

Psalm 62:11 *"God has spoken once, Twice I have heard this: That power belongs to God."*

We pray that our mission will not end, and that all of God's plans for us will become a reality, our testimonies will not vanish and our calling will not die, in the name of Jesus. As we commit our works to The Lord, our plans will be established. We pray that the Lord will direct our steps for His mission for our lives. May God's hands be evident in all areas of our lives, may He perform wonders that cannot be fathomed, and miracles that cannot be counted, in the name of Jesus. John 20:21 *"Then said Jesus to them again, Peace be unto you: as my Father hath sent me, even so send I you."* May the Lord give us peace like a river, a vision for God's assignment, grant us passion for His commission, we shall have love for God's will. Father help us be obedient to Your call, in the name of Jesus.

In this season, may the Lord grant us good works that will produce dumbfounding testimonies that will cause others to ask about our God, for His glory, in Jesus name. May God grant us favor that will cause all those that have looked down on us to be shocked by God's goodness in our lives. And wherever our name is mentioned, we'll obtain uncommon favor this season, uncommon and unprecedented favor shall rest upon our lives, in Jesus name. AMEN.

WHAT IS IN THE NAME THAT IS ABOVE EVERY NAME?

If you want to get to know a person, you start with knowing the person's name. A name conveys the very character and nature of a person.

God's name represents His attributes. His name is a statement of who He is. God has a name for every situation you encounter in life.

Each of His many names reveals His ability, love, power and purposes.

Everyone of God's name in the OT, is wrapped up in Jesus in the NT. For He is God in the flesh. He said if you have seen me, you have seen the Father.

His VERY NAME declares His Divinity.

Some of those names include: The Son of Man, our High Priest, He is God, The Rock, Savior, Mighty God, Lord of All, King of Kings, The Word of God, Light of the World, The Good Shepherd, Head of the church, The Redeemer, The Resurrection and the Life, Bread of Life, The Living Water, The Son of God, Alpha and Omega, Lamb of God, Messiah, Immanuel God with us, Wonderful, Counselor, Mighty God, Everlasting Father, Prince of Peace. Something happens when you call Jesus. One and only, All Powerful, gracious, full of mercies and compassionate God. Change happens when you call Him Healer, Deliverer, your Defender, Provider, Keeper, and the only Way Maker. He is Dependable and Faithful. Willing to come and sup with all that will let Him in and make the impossible possible.

- The power of all of God's names is in Jesus.
- I don't know what you going through, God has a name for it. If you know the name Jesus, demons in hell can't overcome you.
- When we pray in His name, we pray with All authority and power of Jesus.

John 17:26 *"I have made Your name known to them and will make it known..."* Jesus is saying I have revealed who You are, through Your name... Miracle Worker, Deliverer, Healer, Way Maker, Compassionate God.

The Power to make God's glory known is in the name of Jesus.

Isaiah 9:6 *"And His name shall be called Wonderful, Counselor, The mighty God, The Everlasting Father, The Prince of Peace."*

As the Son of God, Jesus was the most exalted person to ever walk the earth. In Philippians 2:10-11 *"Therefore God also has highly exalted Him and given Him the name which is above every name, that at the name of Jesus every knee should bow, of those in heaven, and of those on earth, and of those under the earth, and that every tongue should confess that Jesus Christ is Lord, to the glory of God the Father."*

There are three realms at the name of Jesus; everything in those realms must bow: those in heaven, angels and saints, those on the earth, people, presidents, kings and queens, under the earth Satan and his demons. They all submit to that name; it is the name that causes Satan to back off and crumble. Whether he likes it or not, he has no choice when that name is mentioned. That name, Jesus, is the power that Satan cannot resist.

As you explore the richness contained in the names of Jesus, you will learn to trust the Lord's goodness, rely on His promises, and live in His abundance.

Psalm 124:8 *"Our help is in the name of the Lord, Who made heaven and earth."* He is our Support, Deliverer, Comfort, Helper, Defender and Maker. He Is our life!

The name Jesus produces results like no other name:

- Our guilt and shame have been nailed to the cross.

- Our mind is renewed and we have the mind of Christ. Old things are passed away; all things have become new.

- In that name we are transformed into children of God.

- When we are weak, we are made strong.

- We can come boldly to the Throne of Grace that we may obtain mercy and find grace to help in time of need.

- Because of the name we have assurance of entering into The Lord's presence for all eternity, and hear, "Well done good and faithful servant, enter into the joy of your master."

- Discovery of this name will bring recovery…

When you have that name, you don't have to have silver or gold: It was just the name of Jesus that did the miracle at the beautiful gate.

Acts 3:6-9 Peter and John went to the temple to pray, there was a lame man, crippled from birth, who was put there to beg money. When he saw Peter and John he asked for money. *"Then Peter said, "Silver and gold I do not have, but what I do have I give you: In the name of Jesus Christ of Nazareth, rise up and walk." And he took him by the right hand and lifted him up, and immediately his feet and ankle bones received strength. So he, leaping up, stood and walked and entered the temple with them—walking, leaping, and praising God. And all the people saw him walking and praising God."*

Peter said, "I don't have what you want, but I have what you need, through the power in the name of Jesus Christ of Nazareth, rise up and walk." In that name you can rise from every bondage, shame, limitation, delay, demonic attack…Paul said the same thing to the Philippians 4:19 *"My God shall supply all your needs, according to His riches and glory by Christ Jesus."* This lame man who had been at the mercy of others to help him move, was now able to walk into the temple, and he started walking and leaping (jumping, bouncing, rejoicing) and praising the Lord. If there was anybody there that did not know his story, they might have judged him, saying why is he worshiping so loudly, acting so undignified, why is he worshiping so shamelessly? Only he knows what God has done for him. Sometimes when people do not know, what God has done for you, they tend to judge your outrageous worship. Don't worry, it is for God.

Peter explained what happened: Act 3:16 *"Through faith in the name of Jesus, this man was healed—and you know how crippled he was before. Faith in Jesus' name has healed him before your very eyes."* His miracle was undeniable, undisputed and unquestionable.

Never be ashamed to publicly bless the Lord for His goodness in your life. After Uzzah died from touching the Ark. That is what David did in 2 Samuel 6:12-16, *"So David went and brought up the Ark of God from the house of Obed-Edom to the City of David with gladness. And so it was, when those bearing the Ark of the Lord had gone six paces, that he sacrificed oxen and fatted sheep. Then David danced before the Lord with all his might; and David was wearing a linen ephod. So David and all the house of Israel brought up the Ark of the Lord with shouting and with the sound of the trumpet. Now as the Ark of the Lord came into the City of David, Michal, Saul's daughter, looked through a window and saw King David leaping and whirling before the Lord; and she despised him in her heart."*

V. 20 *"And Michal the daughter of Saul came out to meet David, and said, 'How glorious was the king of Israel today, uncovering himself today in the eyes of the maids of his servants, as one of the base fellows shamelessly uncovers himself!'"*

I like David's reply, V. 21-22 David said to Michal, *"It was before the Lord, who chose me rather than your father or anyone from his house when he appointed me ruler over the Lord's people Israel—I will celebrate before the Lord. I will become even more undignified than this, and I will be humiliated in my own eyes."* Wow, what a grateful heart, what a humble spirit. Psalms 34:1-3 *"I will bless the Lord at all times; His praise shall continually be in my mouth. My soul shall* make its boast in the Lord; The humble shall hear of it and be glad. Oh, magnify the Lord with me, And let us exalt His name together." Bless the Lord O my soul, All That is within me bless His Holy name. We are created to praise God, without reservation, no matter what it looks like. God should be our audience of God, at all time. He is worthy of it all.

David like all the great men of the Bible, knew the power in blessing, exulting and magnifying the name of the Lord:

- Psalm 145:21 *"My mouth will speak the praise of the LORD, And all flesh will bless His holy name forever and ever."*

- Daniel 2:20 Daniel said, *"Let the name of God be blessed forever and ever, For wisdom and power belong to Him."*

The name "Jesus" can be translated several ways: Jesus is the Greek version of the Hebrew name *Yeshua*, which means "salvation."

All that God did through His name in the Old Testament is what He does, in the name of Jesus, in the New Testament. Colossians 1:15 *"He is the image of the invisible God."*

- We can do without a lot of things, but we cannot do without the name of Jesus. It is all powerful; heaven responds to that name. What set the disciples apart from all the other Jews was: They had the name of Jesus. They had the power in the name. Their identity was in the name.

- The early church baptized in that name and did exploit in the name. They were told do what you want, but stop using the name of Jesus, in Acts 4.

- The disciples were willing to be persecuted, suffer and even die for that name.

- God's name is important: If I am your friend, I will know your name; if you need me when you are injured, I can play a nurse and put a bandage on you, if you need money to make up your rent money, I can help, but a man's resources is limited, but God is limitless…

God told Moses, *"Abraham your father knew me as the Almighty God."* Genesis 17:1, 28:3, 35:11, 48:3, 49:25. He kept describing Himself as The Almighty.

- He showed up at the desert for Hagar as Jehovah Roi.

- He was peace for Gideon, Judges 6, with the Midianites.

- For Ruth, He was her kinsman redeemer.

- For David He was The Shepherd.

- Solomon – wisdom and riches.

- Jehoshaphat – He was Jehovah Nissi who fights his battle.

- For Esther – He was the favor that made their enemy their footstool.

- For Prophet Isaiah – He was the eye of eagle to see 700 years ahead and told about Jesus. Isaiah 9:6 *"For unto us a child is born, unto us a son is given: and the government shall be upon his shoulder: and his name shall be called Wonderful, Counselor, The mighty God, The Everlasting Father, The Prince of Peace."*

- Jeremiah was known by God from his mother's womb and chosen for a great purpose. To speak what God says.

- For Ezekiel to prophesy to dry bone and give life.

- For Daniel to display that His God was the Most-High to a pagan nation.

- Mary – Mother of Jesus, that He can use anybody to birth greatness.

- For Peter and Paul, He showed Himself as a God of another chance. The next thing God does in your life will be better than the last.

All Powerful Name:

Psalm 62:11 *"God has spoken once; Twice I have heard this: That power belongs to God."*

My name will be known in all the earth.

God told Moses, I am not a God of one area, like the idol gods of Egypt, the god of futility, god of crops, vengeance, god of sun, god of motherhood… He told Moses, I Am whatever you need, I will be.

I Am about to show an aspect of Me that you need. The I Am, The God who gave you another chance, the deliverer, the cloud by day and fire by night, the water in the rock, the One who make bitter waters sweet. God is able to turn the bitterness in your life to sweetness if you know His name. God became their protector, and their source. He was everything they needed.

I Am, is the fullness of His nature.

Before God demonstrates His power, He introduces Himself. In the beginning God, Genesis 1:1, Before Egypt submission, *"I Am."*

There is security and protection in the name.

It reminds me of the rabbit in the bush story. The hunter was standing looking around, out of nowhere comes this fluffy rabbit that ran and sat between his legs, and he looked up and he saw a weasel burst out of the bush. As this predator saw the rabbit next to a man, it froze in its tracks and backed off.

Proverbs 18:10 *"The name of the Lord is a strong tower; The righteous run to it and are safe."* When in trouble call Jesus, when you face demonic attack, call Jesus.

Trust in the name: *"Some trust in chariots and some in horses, but we trust in the name of the Lord our God."* (Psalm 20:7)

Salvation is in the name: *"For there is no other name under heaven given among men by which we must be saved."* (Acts 4:12)

We must pray in the name of Jesus to get result: *"Until now you have asked nothing in My name. Ask, and you will receive, that your joy may be full."* (John 16:24).

There is power in the name of Jesus when we link our faith with heaven.

On a more humorous note, the news reporter, Paul Harvey, told the story of a three-year-old boy at the grocery store with his mother. She sternly told him before entering the store, *"No chocolate chip cookies, so don't even ask!"* In the store she put him in the little child's seat in the cart, and they wheeled down the aisles. He was quiet until he got to the cookie aisle. He saw those delicious chocolate chip cookies, and he stood up and said, *"Mom, can I have the chocolate chip cookies?"* With a strong voice she said to him, *"I told you not to even ask. No!"*

He sat down. They went down the aisles, but later, the mom had to come back to the cookie aisle again. He asked for them again. She told him, *"Sit down and be quiet. I said no."* Finally arriving at the checkout lane, the little boy knew it was his last chance. He had to do something quick. So he stood up in his seat and shouted as loud as he could, *"In the name of Jesus, may I have some chocolate chip cookies?"*

Everyone around him began to laugh and applaud that little boy. And because of the generosity of the other shoppers, the little boy and his mother left the grocery store with twenty-three boxes of chocolate chip cookies! He was very happy. God loves to answer persistent prayers that are prayed in the name of Jesus. This may be a funny story but let's not forget the message. There is an authority attached to using the name of Jesus.

Value the name: Matthew 6:9, where He said, *"In this manner, therefore, pray: 'Our Father in heaven, Hallowed be Your name.'"*

1 Kings 8:27-29 Solomon, during the temple dedication, he said, *"The heavens cannot contain You, Your name shall be in this house, that as we pray in Your name, You will manifest."* God's name is where He manifests and shows up. It is where He reveals His presence. Yes, God is Omnipresent. But when we gather in His name, when we call His name, we have His attention. We get the attention of Almighty God. Matthew 18:20 *"For where two or three are gathered together in my name, there am I in the midst of them."*

- Jesus said all authority belongs to Him. This name causes heaven to respond, and He has given it to us.

We can bind and lose, decree and declare, in that name, we can pray and the sick will be healed. All you need is the name of Jesus. John 14:14 *"If you ask anything in My name, I will do it."*

- *"Repent, and let every one of you be baptized in the name of Jesus Christ for the remission of sins; and you shall receive the gift of the Holy Spirit."* (Acts 2:38).

- Ephesians 5:20 *"Giving thanks always for all things to God the Father in the name of our Lord Jesus Christ."*

- Paul said this name is so important, do everything you do in that name: The name "Jesus" represents more than the name of any man. His perfection, His position and His praise.

- Do all in His name: Colossians 3:17. *"And whatever you do in word or deed, do all in the name of the Lord Jesus, giving thanks to God the Father through Him."*

- Remembering this great name will keep you from sin. Psalm 119:55 *"I remember Your name in the night, O Lord, And I keep Your law."*

- We are enabled: God's abilities are revealed through His name: *"The people that do know their God shall be strong, and do exploits."* (Daniel 11:32)

- Mark 16:17-18 *"And these signs will follow those who believe: In My name they will cast out demons; they will speak with new tongues; they will take up serpents; and if they drink anything deadly, it will by no means hurt them; they will lay hands on the sick, and they will recover."*

There were six men who went to the hospital to pray for their friend. After praying nothing happened; they went out of the room and started whispering Jesus, Jesus, Jesus. They went back in and kept saying the name louder and louder and the man got up and got dressed. It is the name that will produce your miracle.

The Seventy Return with Joy:

- Luke 10:17 *"Then the seventy returned with joy, saying, "Lord, even the demons are subject to us in Your name."...they submit to that name."*

The name of Jesus brought deliverance from demonic powers. Spiritual wickedness in high places, hear the name of Jesus, and be cast out of our lives now, in mighty name of Jesus Christ.

Constant irritation: When the devil is constantly poking you with the same issue, attack, frustrations: When the demon-possessed girl was loud, irritating and distractive to Paul, in Acts 16:18 *"And this she did for many days. But Paul, greatly annoyed, turned and said to the spirit, 'I command you in the name of Jesus Christ to come out of her.'" And he came out that very hour."*

MAN AT THE BEACH STORY:

I saw this testimony of a man that used to be a witch. He said all the witches in the world would come to a place annually to have their meeting. One night they were having their meeting at the beach. I think he said somewhere in Chicago. Then this one man came, and was walking up and down the beach, praying. He stepped on one of the witches foot, because he could not see them, but they could see him. So that witch told another witch, who told him, go and slap him. So, this witch went and slapped this Christian man that was walking back and forth praying. This man felt the slap, but could not see what hit him, he then cried out loud, "JESUS." This man that was giving the testimony—his name is Omoobajesu—he said sparks came out of his mouth, when he yelled JESUS, went up to the sky, and immediately there came down chariots, fire, and all kinds of warriors and all kinds of ammunition, so they all scatted and their meeting did not hold that night. He said wherever they held their meeting every year, there is great disaster that happens in that region, both natural and man-made that would cost a lot of money, with many lives lost. But all that was prevented because of this one man, who was praying on the beach, and called out the name of JESUS. I always wonder if that man knew what God did through him, in the realm of the spirit. I wondered if God told him to go to the beach that night to pray, and he did not know why, but just obeyed and much destruction was prevented. God is so good! There is power in the name of Jesus!

- Matthew 8:16 *"When evening had come, they brought to Him many who were demon-possessed. And He cast out the spirits with a word, and healed all who were sick."*

   Lord every power possessing my life that is not of You, let them all be cast out, with the Word of God let every satanic plan, affliction and evil be cast out. Lord you healed all who were sick, I now receive healing, in the name of Jesus.

   Let everything that God is, everything that His name represents, manifest in my life, let His glory manifest in all my situations. Amen!

- Where you are despised you shall be raised there.

   Zechariah 3:4 *"Then He answered and spoke to those who stood before Him, saying, 'Take away the filthy garments from him.' And to him He said, 'See, I have*

> *removed your iniquity from you, and I will clothe you with rich robes.'"*

From today, Father God, let every garment that represents filth be taken away from my life. Lord remove iniquity from me and clothe me with a rich robe, in Jesus name.

Everything! Your future is bound up in your name; everything that is likely to happen to you is embedded in that name.

Moses was called Moses, according to Exodus 2, because he was drawn out of water.

For the rest of his life, water played a significant role in his life. He changed water to blood in Exodus chapter 7; he parted the red sea in Exodus, Chapter 14; he turned bitter water to sweet water, in Exodus chapter 15; He brought water out of the rock in Exodus chapter 17, and when he failed to get to the promised land, it is because of water. In Numbers 20, water kept following him.

The Almighty God knows the importance of name, so much that on several occasions, He had to change the names of some people for their destiny to be fulfilled.

When God changed a person's name and gave him a new name, it was usually to establish a new identity.

Genesis 17: 1 -9 He changed Abram to Abraham, a barren man to the father of nations. He changed Sarai to Sarah, (Exodus 17: 15-16) a barren woman, to a princess and mother of nations.

Genesis 32: 24-26: he changed Jacob to Israel; he changed a man to a nation.

Why did God choose new names for some people? The Bible doesn't give us His reasons, but perhaps it was to let them know they were destined for a new mission in life. The new name was a way to let them in on the divine plan and also to assure them that God's plan would be fulfilled in them.

"I'll make a great nation of your descendants, I'll bless you, and I'll make your reputation great, so that you will be a blessing." (Genesis 12:2)

Moving to the New Testament, we see Jesus telling Simon, His new disciple, *"You are Simon the son of John; you shall be called Peter."* (John 1:42). The significance was that the Greek word translated Peter is *petros*, which means "rock." Soul, to Paul.

In Scripture, a name often connotes purpose, authority, make-up, and character. In fact, a person's name is frequently seen as an equivalent of that person.

When Jesus said, *"I have made Your name known to them, and will make it known."* (John 17:26), He was referencing more than just sounds put together in a word. In Jesus, God came to earth in the flesh and unveiled His heart, mind, will, character, and being through the revelation of the name Jesus.

God has exalted His name. In fact, He says in Malachi 1, *"I have a great name, and My name is to be feared."* So, God makes a big deal about His name.

Some scriptures about the names of The Lord:

Psalm 124:8 *"Our help is in the name of the Lord, Who made heaven and earth."*

Colossians 1:15 *"He is the image of the invisible God."*

Acts 19:15 *"And the evil spirit answered and said, 'Jesus I know, and Paul I know; but who are you?'"*

Then He said, "Do not draw near this place. Take your sandals off your feet, for the place where you stand *is* holy ground." Moreover He said, "I *am* the God of your father—the God of Abraham, the God of Isaac, and the God of Jacob." And Moses hid his face, for he was afraid to look upon God.

- Proverbs 18:10 *"The name of the Lord is a strong tower; The righteous run to it and are safe."*

- Psalm 20:7 *"Some trust in chariots and some in horses, but we trust in the name of the Lord our God."*

- *"For there is no other name under heaven given among men by which we must be saved."* (Acts 4:12)

- John 16:24 *"Until now you have asked nothing in My name. Ask, and you will receive, that your joy may be full."*

- Matthew 6:9, where He said, *"In this manner, therefore, pray: 'Our Father in heaven, Hallowed be Your name.'"*

- Matthew 18:20 *"For where two or three are gathered together in my name, there am I in the midst of them."*

- Acts 2:38-39 Then Peter said to them, *"Repent, and let every one of you be baptized in the name of Jesus Christ for the remission of sins; and you shall receive the gift of the Holy Spirit. For the promise is to you and to your children, and to all who are afar off, as many as the Lord our God will call."*

- Mark 16:17-18 *"And these signs will follow those who believe: In My name they will cast out demons; they will speak with new tongues; they will take up serpents; and if they drink anything deadly, it will by no means hurt them; they will lay hands on the sick, and they will recover."*

- Luke 10:17 *"Then the seventy returned with joy, saying, 'Lord, even the demons are subject to us in Your name.'"*

- Isaiah 55:6. *"Seek the Lord while He may be found, Call upon Him while He is near."*

- John 14:6 *"Jesus answered, 'I am the way and the truth and the life. No one comes to the Father except through me.'"*

Just the mention of that precious name can speak peace to the troubled, comfort to the hurting, give life to the dead, joy to the sad, hope for the hopeless and glory to the saved soul.

Do you need Him this today? He is as close as the mention of His name.

Isaiah 55:6. *"Seek the Lord while He may be found, Call upon Him while He is near."*

John 14:6 *"Jesus answered, 'I am the way and the truth and the life. No one comes to the Father except through me.'"*

Then you, too, can enjoy complete access to the Father through the powerful name of Jesus.

It doesn't matter how big your problem is, how bad your sickness is or how powerful your demons are. All are under Jesus' feet. The victory is yours. Just claim it in the name of Jesus.

WHAT DO YOU DO WHEN LIFE SEEMS UNFAIR?

What do you do when everybody you know is getting what you want, and it is not happening for you? Has God forgotten you? Is He not hearing your prayer?

I believe God wants us to trust Him in the mist of delay and unfairness. He knows how to turn things around for His glory.

When God is pleased with our priorities He promises to empower, guide and enable us to enjoy His supernatural blessings. Let us learn key principles of participating in God's bountiful blessings.

1 Samuel 1:1-11, 19-28

Hannah was the first wife of Elkanah, who may have felt he could no longer continue without a child, so he married Peninnah, who had children for him.

Peninnah was the one having all the children. For this, Peninnah taunted and teased Hannah until Hannah couldn't take it any longer.

Year after year, Hannah went to Ephraim to Shiloh, about 15 miles journey; she went to where God is. The power in our prayer is our commitment to go where God is. Hannah's devotion was unwavering. The longer we wait on God, the better our prospective.

Hannah now has God's viewpoint, a better picture of the kingdom's need, she can now see from God's lens, her eyes was opened to see what was going on in the temple.

Eli the Priest was ageing; his sons, who ministered as priests, were filled with all kinds of evil: greed, immorality, there was no fear of God in their hearts. Hannah saw a vacuum in the priesthood. Eli's sons were there, yet there was no real priest of God to take over from Eli. "'Ah!' she cried. 'What can I do?'"

Beyond her barrenness, Hannah saw the need in God's house. "How can I meet that need?" she asked herself. "Oh, if God could give me a male child to be groomed to take over from Eli, so that God's people would be served." So, she made a vow to this end, because she could see the bigger picture.

Peninnah, Hannah's rival provoked her severely to cause her inner tumult and pain, over and over again. But Hannah persisted even though it was a long journey. She persisted even though her rival troubled her and her situation persisted. The answer to Hannah's prayer was in her persistence and in her vow. In our prayer life, there is a place for making a vow; we know that God will keep His end of the deal, because God cannot lie, He does what He says. His word is forever settled in heaven. But as for man, when God gives us what we ask for, we forget our vows sometimes.

While at Shiloh, Hannah prayed through her shame. She prayed through her disgrace. She prayed through her aching heart and sorrowful spirit. She prayed so fervently that the priest thought she was drunk because while she was praying her mouth moved, but no sound come out. She was praying to the God, who sees the heart.

Hannah's prayers had a vow with integrity; she vowed it with the determination to carry it out. In Numbers 30:13, if her husband hears the vow, he has the right to nullify it, so Hannah just moved her mouth, but there was no sound coming from her mouth that anyone could hear; no one could hear her prayers and vow to God. Even the priest could not hear her. She did not take a chance that her vow could be nullified. Sometimes the prayers that you offer to God are only for God's ear only; you can't tell everybody everything. Sometimes we tell people our petition thinking we are on the same team, but they are the really not on the same team and they begin to work in their own cruel way to nullify the promise of God in your life. Sometimes you have to be quiet; you do not have to say everything till they come to pass.

You have to be able to trust in the faithfulness of God, just like Hannah. Every time God opened a closed womb in the Bible, a great character was born. (Ill. *Isaac, Joseph, Samson, Samuel, John the Baptist.*)

Hannah got answer to her prayer because she was willing to follow through. Some of us make vows and forget to follow through after God answers those prayers. After she had the child, she nourished the child, nurtured the child, and weaned the child. Then she went all the way back to Shiloh to meet God again, this time with her little boy, this great gift of God that has caused the whole village to no longer look down on her, she was no longer called barren. He was the evidence, having this little boy, because of this little boy,

Peninnah could no longer insult her about being barren. Now she has this evidence that God has done it for her. But now she is giving him back to God.

She then took him to the temple and told Eli, "This is the child I prayed for." When God answers our prayer, we can tell somebody that God answers prayer.

I am the one that was here earlier. I was broken down, in shame, pain, discouraged, and I made a vow that if God will move in my situation, and bless me with a male child, I will give him back, so here he is. Let him serve you in the work of the Lord. And she returns home alone, going back home without a child. She must have really trusted the faithfulness of God. Even though she had a son, she goes back to live like she had none. The result of this sacrifice was five additional children, besides being the mother of one of the greatest prophet/priests of that time. If Hannah could break her barrenness, you can too. Align your motives with God's. Take a sacrificial vow. Ask the Lord in faith and prepare for a change.

Ask God to grant that every cause of barrenness in every area of your life, to start to produce great fruit, in Jesus name. "Barrenness" means being unproductive as well as being unfruitful. There were several women in the Bible who were barren in the womb and even though they didn't have children at first, they eventually did have children. Such women include Sarah, Rebekah, Rachel, Hannah in the Old Testament, and Elizabeth in New Testament. God worked their barrenness for His greatest good.

When the priest realized what Hannah was doing, he blessed her. Hannah went her way and worshiped God even before her son was born. We should do the same. We are tremendously blessed when we begin to thank God, even before the manifestation takes place.

There are several things that deserve special attention in Hannah's story:

- When we worship God, it is a down payment on that thing we have been praying for.

- Notice that Hannah never lashed out at Peninnah, the other wife. What she did is what we should do. She prayed to God who could handle her situation.

- Notice that Hannah prayed not a generic prayer. She did not pray for material things. She did not pray a "Bless Me Prayer." She did not pray for a child. Instead, she prayed a specific prayer that God would give her a son just for the service of God.

- Often, we beat around the bush for what we want. While God can sort out our requests, He wants us to pray for the exact thing we want. Hannah did just that.

- Notice that Hannah went so far as to say she would dedicate her son to the temple. Hannah was willing to give the first fruit of her womb, and God blessed Hannah's barrenness to the point of giving her three additional sons after Samuel and two daughters. Here we have a woman who was barren when we first read about her, but God brought purpose to her barrenness. God had a purpose for Hannah's barrenness. And certainly, He has a purpose for your barrenness as well.

When Hannah was praying for a son, she was responding to a purpose God had already placed within her. God has placed a purpose in each one of us, and nothing we do will ever satisfy us until the purpose is fulfilled. Hannah wanted a son not for herself, but Hannah knew within her heart of hearts that her son would be instrumental in doing work for God.

> Hannah wanted a baby for a higher purpose. Hannah's purpose was tied to her son's purpose. Her son's purpose was tied to the purpose of so many others, because at the time Israel was also barren.
>
> Hannah's desire to have a son was to bring about God's ultimate's plan. God needed someone special, that He could work though to bring forth a prophet.
>
> God allowed Hannah to be temporarily barren, so He could bring a greater blessing to Israel when the time was right. Your temporary dryness is for a greater good, if you will trust God with it and find His will in your situation.
>
> You might be going through a period of temporarily barrenness right now. Know that God is in charge of your barrenness. Know that God is working things out for your greatest good, His greatest good, the greatest good of those around you and His kingdom.

Samuel was dedicated to the temple as Hannah had promised. After he was weaned around the age of 3 years, Hannah took him to the temple to live with Eli at Shiloh, where it all started. Samuel became a prophet, priest and judge. Samuel was the one who anointed Saul, the first king of Israel. He was the one who anointed David whose lineage continued through Jesus Christ.

Part of Hannah's story is in all of us. For you see, we are all barren or have been barren in some area of our lives. Since "barrenness" is the absence of fruit, if you are not bearing fruit in any area of your life, then you are barren.

If you are not producing fruit in your church, you are barren. If you are not producing fruit in your ministry, you are barren. If you are not producing fruit in your marriage, you are barren.

Galatians 5:22-23 gives us the nine fruits of the Spirit. If you don't have love and if you are not loving, then you are barren. If you know deep down within, you are barren in the love department, acknowledge that and begin reading everything in the Bible about love, because God is love, and whoever abides in love, abides in God, and God in him. (1 John 4:16b NIV).

If you don't have joy, then you are barren. If you don't have peace, then you are barren. Acknowledge your area of spiritual barrenness, pray about it, find God's grace, and worship.

I'm reminded now of what Jesus did to the fig tree that was full of leaves, yet it wasn't bearing fruit. In other words, the tree was barren. Jesus cursed the fig tree. You don't have to be cursed. You, like Hannah, can be blessed instead.

If you are barren now, it is for God's purpose.

We should pray to God fervently like Hannah because James tells us that the effectual fervent prayer of the righteous availeth much. (James 5:16)

The Bible mentions only one New Testament woman who was barren, and like Hannah, she was barren for God's purpose.

Elizabeth and her husband Zechariah prayed for a male child. The devout couple couldn't understand how they were serving God, yet they were childless. However, in the fullness of time, Elizabeth did conceive, and her son's name was John. We know him as John the Baptist. God could have opened up her womb and given her a child long before He did, but God had a purpose for Elizabeth's barrenness.

God opened up Elizabeth's womb to have a baby at the right time so John the Baptist would be the forerunner of Jesus Christ. This wouldn't have worked had John the Baptist been born early or later. Jesus said, in Matthew 11:11 *""Assuredly, I say to you, among those born of women there has not risen one greater than John the Baptist."*

God had a purpose for Jesus to come to earth when He did. Israel was barren and had expected the coming Messiah long before He came. It was in the fullness of time that Jesus was born of the Virgin Mary.

Your barrenness can be turned into blessings. Trust that God will use your barrenness for your greatest good.

Acknowledge your barrenness. Pray like Hannah to God's ears and leave the final results up to God.

WHO GOD IS IN MY LIFE?

He is The Controller of heaven and the earth. The Hope of Glory, The Great I Am, The Wonderful Father. God is the Creator and Sustainer of the Universe.

Psalm 18:30 *"As for God, his way is perfect: the word of the Lord is tried: he is a buckler to all those that trust in him."*

May the Lord do for me what no man can do. May He do what will shock my enemies, because He is God. May He promote me above anyone's expectation. May God fight my hidden battles and grant victory in all areas. May His eyes of mercy shine upon me and may He send me help from His sanctuary. May the Lord deliver me from every evil plan. May the Lord arise and let my enemies be scattered. Lord arise and cause every battle of my life to be scattered. May God plead my cause in all areas by giving me justice and vindication where there has been unfairness and injustice. Father remove shame and reproach trying to rule my life. May You break every spell and curse, jinx, evil covenant and enchantment that has been working against me, causing trouble in my life to end, in the mighty name of Jesus.

Lord deliver me from sinful habits. May You arise and destroy all forms of worldliness, carnality, and whatever is causing me to compromise, in Jesus name. Give me a life that honors You. I pray for a fresh anointing to do spectacular exploits and be successful in all areas. May God give me double glory in all areas of shame. I pray that The Lord will move me from labor to favor, in Jesus name. May He turn my story to glory. Let God arise and turn all my struggles to success, ridicules to respect, and obstacles into opportunities. Lord I am Yours, make me an instrument in Your hands, in Jesus mighty name. Amen

100 TO DEAL WITH ISSUES OF LIFE

1. Isaiah 50:4 *"The Lord God has given Me The tongue of the learned, That I should know how to speak A word in season to him who is weary. He awakens Me morning by morning, He awakens My ear To hear as the learned."*

2. Zephaniah 3:17 *"The Lord your God in your midst, The Mighty One, will save; He will rejoice over you with gladness, He will quiet you with His love, He will rejoice over you with singing."*

3. Zechariah 2:8 *"For thus says the Lord of hosts: 'He sent Me after glory, to the nations which plunder you; for he who touches you touches the apple of His eye.'"*

4. Isaiah 62:3 (NLT) *"The Lord will hold you in his hand for all to see a splendid crown in the hand of God."*

Scriptures to Pray for Victory:

5. Isaiah 54:17 *"No weapon formed against you shall prosper, And every tongue which rises against you in judgment You shall condemn. This is the heritage of the servants of the Lord, And their righteousness is from Me,"* says the Lord.

6. Psalm 25:1-2 *"To You, O Lord, I lift up my soul. O my God, I trust in You; Let me not be ashamed; Let not my enemies triumph over me."*

7. Psalm 35:1-2 *"Plead my cause, O Lord, with those who strive with me; Fight against those who fight against me. Take hold of shield and buckler, And stand up for my help."*

8. Psalm 40:13-14 *"Be pleased, O Lord, to deliver me; O Lord, make haste to help me! 14 Let them be ashamed and brought to mutual confusion Who seek to destroy my life; Let them be driven backward and brought to dishonor Who wish me evil."*

9. Psalm 140:9-10 *"As for the head of those who surround me, Let the evil of their lips cover them; Let burning coals fall upon them; Let them be cast into the fire, Into deep pits, that they rise not up again."*

10. Psalm 121:7-8 *"The Lord shall preserve you from all evil; He shall preserve your soul. The Lord shall preserve your going out and your coming in From this time forth, and even forevermore."*

11. 1 Peter 2:24 *"Who Himself bore our sins in His own body on the tree, that we, having died to sins, might live for righteousness—by whose stripes you were healed."*

12. Psalm 147:3 *"He heals the brokenhearted And binds up their wounds."*

13. Psalm 107:20 *"He sent His word and healed them, And delivered them from their destructions."*

14. Isaiah 58:8 *"Then your light shall break forth like the morning, Your healing shall spring forth speedily, And your righteousness shall go before you; The glory of the Lord shall be your rear guard."*

15. Jeremiah 17:14 *"Heal me, O Lord, and I shall be healed; Save me, and I shall be saved, For You are my praise."*

16. Psalm 30:2 *"O Lord my God, I cried out to You, And You healed me."*

Scriptures for Strength:

17. Isaiah 40:29 *"He gives power to the weak, And to those who have no might He increases strength."*

18. Philippians 4:13 *"I can do all things through Christ who strengthens me."*

19. Psalm 119:28 *"My soul melts from heaviness; Strengthen me according to Your word."*

20. Ephesians 6:10 *"Finally, my brethren, be strong in the Lord and in the power of His might."*

21. Isaiah 40:31 *"But those who wait on the Lord Shall renew their strength; They shall mount up with wings like eagles, they shall run and not be weary, They shall walk and not faint."*

22. Psalm 46:1 *"God is our refuge and strength, A very present help in trouble."*

23. 2 Corinthians 12:9-10 *"And He said to me, 'My grace is sufficient for you, for My strength is made perfect in weakness. Therefore, most gladly I will rather boast in my infirmities, that the power of Christ may rest upon me. Therefore I take pleasure in infirmities, in reproaches, in needs, in persecutions, in distresses, for Christ's sake. For when I am weak, then I am strong.'"*

24. Nehemiah 8:10 *"...Do not grieve, for the joy of the LORD is your strength."*

Scriptures for Finances & Provision:

25. Psalm 34:10 *"The young lions lack and suffer hunger; But those who seek the Lord shall not lack any good thing."*

26. Philippians 4:19 *"And my God shall supply all your need according to His riches in glory by Christ Jesus."*

27. Matthew 6:26 *"Look at the birds of the air, for they neither sow nor reap nor gather into barns; yet your heavenly Father feeds them. Are you not of more value than they?"*

28. Malachi 3:10 *"Bring all the tithes into the storehouse, That there may be food in My house, And try Me now in this,"* Says the Lord of hosts, *"If I will not open for you the windows of heaven And pour out for you such blessing That there will not be room enough to receive it."*

29. Proverbs 10:22 *"The blessing of the Lord makes one rich, And He adds no sorrow with it."*

30. Deuteronomy 8:18 *"And you shall remember the Lord your God, for it is He who gives you power to get wealth, that He may establish His covenant which He swore to your fathers, as it is this day."*

31. 3 John 2 *"Beloved, I pray that you may prosper in all things and be in health, just as your soul prospers."*

Scriptures for The Peace of God:

32. 2 Thessalonians 3:16 *"Now may the Lord of peace Himself give you peace always in every way. The Lord be with you all."*

33. John 16:33 *"These things I have spoken unto you, that in me ye might have peace. In the world ye shall have tribulation: but be of good cheer; I have overcome the world."*

34. Isaiah 26:3 *"Thou wilt keep him in perfect peace, whose mind is stayed on thee: because he trusteth in thee."*

35. Romans 12:18 *"If it be possible, as much as lieth in you, live peaceably with all men."*

36. Romans 15:13 *"Now the God of hope fill you with all joy and peace in believing, that ye may abound in hope, through the power of the Holy Ghost."*

37. Hebrews 12:14 *"Follow peace with all [men], and holiness, without which no man shall see the Lord."*

38. Psalm 4:8 *"I will both lay me down in peace, and sleep: for thou, LORD, only makest me dwell in safety."*

39. Proverbs 12:20 *"Deceit [is] in the heart of them that imagine evil: but to the counselors of peace [is] joy."*

40. 1 Corinthians 14:33 *"For God is not [the author] of confusion, but of peace, as in all churches of the saints."*

Uplifting Scriptures:

41. 2 Corinthians 1:3-4 *"Blessed be the God and Father of our Lord Jesus Christ, the Father of mercies and God of all comfort, who comforts us in all our tribulation, that we may be able to comfort those who are in any trouble, with the comfort with which we ourselves are comforted by God."*

42. Psalm 34:17-18 *"The righteous cry out, and the Lord hears, And delivers them out of all their troubles. The Lord is near to those who have a broken heart, And saves such as have a contrite spirit."*

43. Proverbs 3:5-6 *"Trust in the Lord with all your heart, And lean not on your own understanding; ⁶ In all your ways acknowledge Him, And He shall direct your paths."*

44. Isaiah 41:10 **"***Fear not, for I am with you; Be not dismayed, for I am your God. I will strengthen you, Yes, I will help you, I will uphold you with My righteous right hand.*"

Scriptures for Faith:

45. Genesis 15:6 *"And he [Abraham] believed in the Lord, and He accounted it to him for righteousness."*

46. Genesis 18:14 *"Is anything too hard for the Lord? At the appointed time I will return to you [Abraham], according to the time of life, and Sarah shall have a son."*

47. Numbers 23:19 *"God is not a man, that He should lie, nor a son of man, that He should repent. Has He said, and will He not do? Or has He spoken, and will He not make it good?"*

48. 2 Chronicles 20:20 *"So they rose early in the morning and went out into the Wilderness of Tekoa; and as they went out, Jehoshaphat stood and said, 'Hear me, O Judah and you inhabitants of Jerusalem: Believe in the Lord your God, and you shall be established; believe His prophets, and you shall prosper.'"*

49. Job 22:28 (AMP) *"You will also decide and decree a thing, and it will be established for you; And the light [of God's favor] will shine upon your ways."*

50. Psalm 27:13 *"I would have lost heart, unless I had believed that I would see the goodness of the Lord In the land of the living."*

51. Psalm 145:18 "The LORD is near to all who call on him, to all who call on him in truth."

52. Matthew 18:19 *"Again I say to you that if two of you agree on earth concerning anything that they ask, it will be done for them by My Father in heaven."*

53. Matthew 19:26 *"But Jesus looked at them and said to them, "With men this is impossible, but with God all things are possible."*

54. Mark 5:36 *"As soon as Jesus heard the word that was spoken, He said to the ruler of the synagogue, "Do not be afraid; only believe."*

55. Luke 1:37 (AMP) *"For with God nothing [is or ever] shall be impossible."*

56. Luke 1:45 *"Blessed is she who believed, for there will be a fulfillment of those things which were told her from the Lord."*

57. Acts 16:31 *"So they said, "Believe on the Lord Jesus Christ, and you will be saved, you and your household."*

58. Romans 10:17 *"So then faith comes by hearing, and hearing by the Word of God."*

59. 2 Corinthians 5:7 (NIV) *"For we live by faith, not by sight."*

60. Hebrews 11:1 *"Now faith is the substance of things hoped for, the evidence of things not seen."*

61. Hebrews 11:6 *"But without faith it is impossible to please Him, for he who comes to God must believe that He is, and that He is a rewarder of those who diligently seek Him."*

62. James 4:2 *"Yet you do not have because you do not ask."*

Scriptures for Love:

63. John 3:16 *"For God loved the world in this way: He gave his one and only Son, so that everyone who believes in him will not perish but have eternal life."*

64. Romans 5:8 *"But God proves his own love for us in that while we were still sinners, Christ died for us."*

65. 1 Corinthians 13:8 *"Love never ends. But as for prophecies, they will come to an end; as for tongues, they will cease; as for knowledge, it will come to an end."*

66. 1 Corinthians 13:6 *"Love finds no joy in unrighteousness but rejoices in the truth."*

67. Galatians 5:22 *"But the fruit of the Spirit is love, joy, peace, longsuffering, kindness, goodness, faithfulness."*

68. John 13:35 *"By this shall all men know that ye are My disciples: if ye have love one for another."*

69. 2 Timothy 1:7 *"For God has not given us a spirit of fear, but one of power, love, and sound judgment."*

Scriptures for Tough Times

70. Isaiah 66:9 *"Shall I bring to the time of birth, and not cause delivery?" says the Lord. "Shall I who cause delivery shut up the womb?"* says your God.

71. Romans 8:18 (NLT) *"Yet what we suffer now is nothing compared to the glory he will reveal to us later."*

72. Joshua 1:9 (NLT) *"This is my command—be strong and courageous! Do not be afraid or discouraged. For the Lord your God is with you wherever you go."*

73. Proverbs 31:25 (NIV) *"She is clothed with strength and dignity; she can laugh at the days to come."*

74. Psalm 37:5 (NLT) *"Commit everything you do to the Lord. Trust him, and he will help you."*

75. Isaiah 43:2 (NLT) *"When you go through deep waters, I will be with you. When you go through rivers of difficulty, you will not drown. When you walk through the fire of oppression, you will not be burned up; the flames will not consume you."*

76. Ecclesiastes 3:1 (NLT) *"For everything there is a season, a time for every activity under heaven."*

77. Romans 8:28 (NLT) *"And we know that God causes everything to work together for the good of those who love God and are called according to his purpose for them."*

78. Isaiah 41:10 *"Don't be afraid, for I am with you. Don't be discouraged, for I am your God. I will strengthen you and help you. I will hold you up with my victorious right hand."*

79. Jeremiah 29:11 *"For I know the plans I have for you, plans to prosper you and not harm you, plans to give you hope and a future."*

Scriptures for Forgiveness:

80. Colossians 3:13 *"Bearing with one another and, if one has a complaint against another, forgiving each other; as the Lord has forgiven you, so you also must forgive."*

81. Matthew 6:12 – From the Lord's Prayer – *"And forgive us our debts, as we also have forgiven our debtors."*

82. Psalm 103:10-12 *"He has not dealt with us according to our sins, nor punished us according to our iniquities. For as the heavens are high above the earth, so great is His mercy toward those who fear Him; as far as the east is from the west, so far has He removed our transgressions from us."*

83. Ephesians 1:7-8 *"In Him we have redemption through His blood, the forgiveness of sins, according to the riches of His grace which He made to abound toward us in all wisdom and prudence."*

84. Acts 3:19 *"Repent therefore and be converted, that your sins may be blotted out, so that times of refreshing may come from the presence of the Lord."*

85. Luke 7:47-48 *"Therefore I say to you, her sins, which are many, are forgiven, for she loved much. But to whom little is forgiven, the same loves little."*

86. Matthew 6:14-15 *"For if you forgive men their trespasses, your heavenly Father will also forgive you. But if you do not forgive men their trespasses, neither will your Father forgive your trespasses."*

87. Mark 11:25 *"And whenever you stand praying, if you have anything against anyone, forgive him, that your Father in heaven may also forgive you your trespasses."*

88. Luke 6:37 *"Judge not, and you shall not be judged. Condemn not, and you shall not be condemned. Forgive, and you will be forgiven."*

89. Isaiah 1:18 *"Come now, and let us reason together,"* says the Lord, *"Though your sins are like scarlet, they shall be as white as snow; though they are red like crimson, they shall be as wool."*

90. Isaiah 43:25 *"I, even I, am He who blots out your transgressions for My own sake; and I will not remember your sins."*

91. Isaiah 55:7 *"Let the wicked forsake his way, and the unrighteous man his thoughts; let him return to the Lord, and He will have mercy on him; and to our God, for He will abundantly pardon."*

Scriptures for Marriage:

92. Ephesians 4:2: *"Be completely humble and gentle; be patient, bearing with one another in love."*

93. 1 Peter 4:8: *"Above all, love each other deeply, because love covers over a multitude of sins."*

94. Ephesians 5:25: *"For husbands, this means love your wives, just as Christ loved the church. He gave up his life for her."*

95. Genesis 2:24: *"Therefore a man shall leave his father and his mother and hold fast to his wife, and they shall become one flesh."*

96. Ecclesiastes 4:12: *"Though one may be overpowered, two can defend themselves. A cord of three strands is not quickly broken."*

97. Mark 10:9: *"Therefore what God has joined together, let no one separate."*

98. Romans 12:10: *"Be devoted to one another in love. Honor one another above yourselves."*

99. 1 Peter 4:8: *"Most important of all, continue to show deep love for each other, for love covers a multitude of sins."*

100. Ephesians 5:21: *"Submit to one another out of reverence for Christ."*

150 PRAYER POINTS FOR ALL KINDS OF SITUATIONS

1. I use the blood of Jesus to chase out anything that will sabotage my testimony, in Jesus name.

2. God will be first in all areas of my life. Lord help me to have the right priorities.

3. Anything that is call good, will locate me. You will not lack any good thing.

4. Sickness will not know me. By His strips I am healed. By His words I am made whole.

5. Lord cause my marriage to thrive, let it become enjoyable and full of love, it is sweeter and more fulfilling.

6. God is in your midst, mighty to save. He will rejoice over you with gladness, He will quiet you with love and rejoice over you with singing.

7. God, may You delight in my prosperity.

8. Holy Spirit of God, open my eyes to see beyond the visible to the invisible. Lord let all spiritual blindness end, in the name of Jesus.

9. God instructs me and keeps me as the apple of His eye.

10. Father God, let our enemies make a mistake that will lead to our divine lifting.

11. You have been working, and trying hard to make it, but there are some evil powers swallowing the result of your prayers and hard work. Today it will stop. Pray, command those powers to fall down and perish.

12. May your season of breakthroughs reject evil delays. My breakthrough shall be unchallenged, and unhindered, by the blood of Jesus. I bulldoze my way into breakthrough this month in the name of Jesus.

13. Lord lift me up from the valley I have found myself and take me to the mountain top. IJN Holy Spirit help me pick up my lost glory, in Jesus name.

14. Pray Say Almighty God, this year reveal Your perfect will for my life.

15. Pray for the help of the Holy Spirit, so you don't miss what God has for you this year. He is our helper.

16. We pull down every stronghold of marital failure and marital distress, in the name of Jesus.

17. Degree and declare that this year, will be the year for divine accomplishment, in all areas of life.

18. I declare God's Word about who I am, what I have, and what I can do in Christ Jesus who gives me strength. I am established as His child in all ways and I will arise and shine in His light.

19. I have favor with God and man; the favor of God is speaking on my behalf, in this season.

20. May the Lord frustrate, disappoint and destroy every work of the devil in my life.

21. Throughout this season, the Holy Spirit will help, enable and power me in all my undertaking, in the name of Jesus.

22. I pray every unsaved person in my family will be saved this year by the Great power of God, in Jesus name.

23. Almighty God, just as You use Moses to display Your power, this year use me to display Your power and Your glory.

24. Pray Father bless me with big financial blessing, to be able to bless Your kingdom, with big donation, bless me to be able to sponsor missionaries, bless me to be a great blessing to the poor, Father God, bless me and make me a blessing everywhere I show up, let it be You showing up through me, in the name of Jesus. Father, take all the glory!

25. Father God release Your blessings on my relationships, that I may be married as that is the desires of my heart. May the Lord do it for me, in this season.

26. In this season I shall walk in divine wisdom, intuitive, grace, power, discernment, understanding, and a higher intellectual ability, in the name of Jesus.

27. Lord help me come into a place of purpose, calling and destiny. A place of greater impact. A place of joy, peace and blessings. That the blessed, will see me and call me blessed, in Jesus name I pray.

28. Anybody waiting for my shame, will see my fame. This is the least I will ever be. Amen!

29. I shall not labor in vain. Lord help me, to not to labor in vain, may You bless every work of my hand, in the name of Jesus.

30. What stops people will not stop me, what hinders others, will not hinder me. What affects other negatively will not affect me, for God is my helper.

31. I am set free to enjoy God, honor God, fall in love with Him afresh. I shall love the Lord with all my heart, mind, spirit and soul.

32. Father God set a guard over my mouth, I will speak with wisdom, my words will produce life, all the days of my life, for the glory of God.

33. I am anxious for nothing, but in everything by prayer and supplication with thanksgiving I let my requests be made known

to God. And the peace of God, which surpasses all, is guarding me.

34. By God's grace, I shall finish well, and everything I do, I will finish well.

35. I overcome past weakness and sins; Lord enable me to walk in divine obedience. May the spirit of excellence fall on me; God will give me ability to be outstanding for Him.

36. The blessings of God shall turn every curse in my life to blessings.

37. No more spirit of rejection, I shall not only be accepted, but I shall be celebrated. If God be for me who can be against me?

38. No more stagnancy, I am moving with full speed, to my promise land, to possess my possessions. I will no longer be stuck.

39. No good thing will He withhold from those who walk uprightly, may The Lord not withhold any good thing from me and I shall walk uprightly.

40. What afflicted me in the past will no longer do so. (Nahum 1:9). Many are the afflictions of the righteous, but God will deliver me out of them all, in Jesus' name.

41. We resist the devil, his works and acts in our lives and our families, Satan, we resist and forbid all your involvement in our family affairs, in the name of Jesus.

42. Today, as I pray with the Word of God, angels of God are going to work on my behalf, in Jesus name.

43. Everywhere my name shows up it will receive a positive response and divine favor.

44. May God send me help from His sanctuary. All my helpers shall locate me quickly.

45. Anointing of easy will rest upon me, and make life easy for me in all by undertaking, Jesus name.

46. Health and wholeness shall be my, I am strong in the Lord and in the Power of His mighty.

47. Let the Word of God that is like fire burn everything in my life that is not of God. It is like a hammer that shatters everything that is not like God in my life.

48. You will arise and shine for the glory of the Lord has risen upon you.

49. Holy Spirit, help me to avoid praying amiss; let the words of my mouth and the meditation of my heart be acceptable before God, in Jesus name.

50. I declare by faith that my family and I will be beneficiaries of divine health. By the stripes of Jesus Christ, we are healed from all diseases, in Jesus name.

51. Every power of demotion and downgrading targeted against my destiny, end, in the name of Jesus.

52. Every spirit, power and personality working against my elevation and promotion evaporate, in the name of Jesus.

53. Every ancestral curse working against my destiny, perish, in the name of Jesus.

54. Every power preventing me from enjoying the goodness of the Lord in the land of the living, end, in the name of Jesus.

55. By the thunder and lightning of the Holy Ghost: Lord humiliate every enemy battle array set against me this season! In the name of Jesus.

56. Every evil done against me in the night: I overthrow and overcome it by the blood of Jesus Christ. I win every battle I fight in my dreams; I shall not be a victim in the dream or in the physical realm, in the name of Jesus.

57. The enemy always uses conspiracy to come against God's people: Every conspiracy orchestrated against me in the daytime: scatter unto desolation, in the name of Jesus.

58. Pray, say not by my power, but by the Spirit of the living God, let every great mountain of problems in my life, become a plain, every mountain of pain become a plain, financial mountain go, in the name of Jesus. Poverty, you will not thrive in my life, by God, I shall leap over every financial wall and be financially free, in the name of Jesus. Angels of blessing, locate me now, in the name of Jesus.

59. In the presence of those who call me nobody, may the God of Israel arise, and make me somebody, in the name of Jesus. In the presence of those who are asking who my God is, oh God, arise and manifest Yourself, in the name of Jesus. When

Pharaoh said to Moses, "I know not your God" God showed up. May God show up for me, in the presence of my enemies.

60. You spirit of death and hell, I am not your candidate, Jesus died that, I might live and declare the works of the Lord, by His death, I leap over wall of death, Jesus' resurrection power has given me life abundantly, in the name of Jesus.

61. Tragedy, you shall not locate me, by the great power of God, I am leaping over you, in the name of Jesus

62. Every power, planning to wage war against my divine vision, what are you waiting for, end in the name of Jesus.

63. You my generational greatness buried deep within me, hear the word of the Lord: MANIFEST! In the name of Jesus.

64. Holy Ghost Fire: Convert the camp of my adversaries into desolate wilderness! In the name of Jesus.

65. My life, move from minimum to maximum, in all areas of blessings, in the name of Jesus.

66. Whether the enemy likes it or not, I shall not bow to the devil, in the name of Jesus.

67. LORD let every face of mockery staring and laughing at me: hear the verdict of Miracles that will wipe out my past and present ridicule! In the name of Jesus.

68. Every power caging my divine dreams and vision, fall down and perish. Whatever I am going through is not how my story is going to end, God is working it all out.

69. Anointing to excel, fall upon me now, in the name of Jesus.

70. As from now on, I shall prevail against the delay and limitation to my breakthroughs, in the name of Jesus.

71. Finger of God, write my name in the book of success, in the name of Jesus.

72. Let the rivers of breakthroughs flow into my life, in the name of Jesus.

73. Anointing of sudden change for good, come upon my life. Father God, don't let our story end the way things look now.

74. God has divine promise for your life, pray that God's divine promise and purpose for your life should come to pass this year.

75. Pray say Father God, let everything that has been difficult for me in the past, let them become easy and doable for me, from now on.

76. Father deliver me from those who hate me, cause all their plans against me to backfire. Lord send confusion to their mix, turn them against each other, in Jesus name.

77. Father close the chapter of sorrow in my life and open new chapter of joy, peace and godliness, in the name of Jesus.

78. Lord close every chapter of failure and shame, open chapter of success, favor and blessings.

79. Lord anoint me with the oil of gladness, let my life be filled with Your presence and power, in the name of Jesus.

80. Lord breath upon my hands and let good things start to happen to the work of my hands.

81. From today, let all the doors that has been short against me and my family, Father open them all, in the mighty name of Jesus.

82. Command every spirit of limitation in my life to be destroyed, in the name of Jesus.

83. Pray, Almighty God I dedicate to You my children, take total control of our lives, may we be for signs and wonders, deliver our purpose from bewitchment, do not permit the evil ones to change our destiny, or the destiny of my children, In the name of Jesus.

84. Father God in this season, make us like a plant by the rivers of water, may all areas of our lives be fruitful, may this season be the most fruitful season of our lives, whatever we do, it shall prosper, in the mighty name of Jesus.

85. Pray that God will equip you to solve problems that comes your way, like the good Samaritan, Mary Magdalene, Joseph, and Noah, in the name of Jesus.

86. Almighty God give me a grace to be a good person, because Your son is good, I receive the credit for His goodness, bless me to leave an inheritance to my children, and my children's children, let wealth change hands, I receive by your goodness the wealth of the sinners, in the name of Jesus.

87. Father God, let all the blessings of Abraham be ours, through Jesus Christ, that we might receive the promise of the Spirit through faith, in the name of Jesus.

88. I receive the anointing to be divinely lifted, to excel and prosper in all that I do, I shall excel and prosper in all areas of life, in Jesus name.

89. Almighty God, give me the power to overcome every obstacle, difficulties, hindrance, hurdle, obstructions, to my breakthrough, in Jesus name. Father give me the power to create wealth, power to succeed, Lord grant me the power to make decisions that will produce good result, in the name of Jesus.

90. When God divinely lift you up, all those that have been working against you will not understand it: I pray your unprecedented lifting will cause confusion amongst your enemies in Jesus name.

91. Whatever is hiding my greatness, give way now, get out of my life, in the name of Jesus.

92. . In Jesus' name, I bind and cast out every strongman having my goods, and blessings in His possession.

93. Father as we call upon you today, may You deliver us, from all challenges, break the curse of automatic failure, Lord rebuke failure at the edge of our breakthrough it must come to an end, in the name of Jesus.

94. Father teach me Your ways, so I can have Your treats and attributes, teach me Your character, so I can act like You, give me the mind of Christ so all my action will be like Your action, in the name of Jesus. Lord help me to be like You in all areas of life. You are the only true source of peace, the Prince of Peace, make me what You are, in the name of Jesus.

95. Financial challenge can steal your peace, Pray and forbid every strongman of poverty from ruling in your life...

96. Any power capitalizing on any weakness in my life, expire in the name of Jesus. Every evil family pattern I cancel you by the blood of Jesus, you shall not ruin my life, or the life of my children.

97. Pray for the glory of God to come down, where the glory is there is no evil that can duel there. Pray for the Almighty God to rain His glorious glory upon us today like never before.

98. Lord help us to have peace like never before, we bind everything that is been stealing our peace.

99. Father God, give me the grace to love righteousness, and to hate iniquity and fear You, in the name of God.

100. Goodness and mercy of the Lord envelope my destiny, let who You are cover me, Father wrap Your loving arms around me, in the name of Jesus.

101. Every wall of separation between me and my blessings, collapse by fire, in the name of Jesus.

102. Lord Jesus Christ, by Your blood, I withdraw my case file, my purpose, my blessings, my relationship, my finances, and my life from all evil altars.

103. Every demonic influence over my life and my prayer, be canceled by the power in the blood of Jesus, in the name of Jesus.

104. I stand against every unprofitable work of darkness in my life and in my family, in the name of Jesus. I come against every

satanic molestation in the dream. Lord put a stop to it, by the power in the blood of Jesus. I am a no go zone to the devil, in the name of Jesus.

105. Father give me a revelation of who I am to you, show me how to receive and be confident in my place in You. Thank You Lord for Your unconditional love for me. You are my ABBA Father, in the name of Jesus.

106. By the power of the Holy Ghost, I break and lose myself from all evil power that has been working against my progress and success, working against my mind, working against my family, Father God, deliver me from every power working against the will of God for my life, in Jesus name.

107. Almighty God bring me into a deeper place in You, a place of intimacy with You, Father God don't let me remain stagnant in my walk with You. Let there be an improvement in spiritual life, Lord grant me positive change in my prayer life, release to me, what has been missing in my walk with You, in the name of Jesus.

108. Lord let my point of discomfort turn to a point of comfort, Lord let our point of ridicule be converted to a source of miracle. Father God, may my point of mockery be converted to a source of honor.

109. Lord deliver us and our children from the spirit of error, slip-ups, mistakes, and wrong believe and bad decisions, in Jesus name.

110. Asking is a principle in the education of acquiring wealth. Receiving is always a product of asking. It is your responsibility and privilege to ask God for financial blessing. Therefore today, Lord I ask You to bless me, with money yielding ideas, I pray for wisdom, wisdom creates the path to prosperity.

111. Almighty God, bless me with the type of wisdom that will promote me, grant me wisdom that will announce me, Father give me the wisdom that will open great doors of provision for me and my family, that I may be a blessing everywhere I go, in Jesus name.

112. Father God today I seek divine opportunities and elevation, help me Lord to find them, for your name sake, let me find your blessings like never before, in the name of Jesus.

113. Almighty God, I knock at the door of your resource, supply my need in a supernatural way, Father open to me the doors that has been closed to me, let every door of treasure be open in their own accord, in the mighty name of Jesus.

114. Lord, show me favor in my business, ministry, career and let me be well compensated financially for the work I do, in the name of Jesus.

115. Throughout the year and for the rest of my life, there shall be no financial lack, there shall be no financial dryness or nakedness, in the mighty name of Jesus.

116. Lord, in this season, don't let me suffer financial shame; for my eyes is on You. Father as I look to You, let my face be radiant, let me not be covered with shame. Father end all areas of

shame in my life, replace shame with honor, in the name of Jesus.

117. I reject financial embarrassment, creditors will no longer be harassing me in the name of Jesus, from today, I am delivered from debt, I shall owe no man anything, but to love them. Thank You Lord for financial abundance, thank You Father for financial freedom, Lord thank You for financial overflow, in the mighty name of Jesus.

118. Father grant me the power to be fulfilled, power to be successful, and prosperous, in the name of Jesus.

119. Beginning from this hour, the God of wealth and riches goes to work in my life and finances. Let new chapter of business opportunity opens for me, an amazing career be offered to me, in the name of Jesus.

120. I command every spell and enchantment against my financial destiny to be forever destroyed, the devour shall no longer have power over my finances, the thief can no longer steal from me, and the killer shall not kill my financial blessings, in Jesus name.

121. By the great power of God, this year, my financial blessing and financial breakthrough, shall be unstoppable, in Jesus name. Psalm 23:1 *"The Lord is my shepherd; I shall not want."* Nothing missing, I shall be satisfied and fulfilled, in Jesus name.

122. No force in hell can stop what God is out to do in my life this season, He is moving me forward, in Jesus name.

123. As you give, God will begin to pour His blessing upon you. As you use your talents and skills, through the Power of the Holy Spirit, His blessing will multiply beyond anything you can think or imagine, that God has for you, in Jesus name.

124. Lord You, revealed Your arm to me, that I might know and trust Your strength and power. Father help me not to look at my situation, but to keep my eyes on Your ability and power, in the name of Jesus.

125. Wherever satanic agents are gathered against me, your time is up, be scattered unto desolation, fail in all your plans against me, in the name of Jesus.

126. Lord open my eyes and turn it from darkness, to light, deliver my life from the power of Satan, to the power of God, through the blood of Jesus. Grant me forgiveness of sins and an inheritance among those who are sanctified by faith, in Jesus name.

127. Lord Jesus give me power over unclean spirits to cast them out of my life, to cast out all kinds of sickness and disease, in the name of Jesus.

128. I release the power and authority of the Word against ALL demonic encounter, in the name of Jesus.

129. LORD, release Your powerful voice, may the voice of God speak into my life, Lord speak to my situation, by Your great voice, and change my story for good, in the name of Jesus.

130. In the name of Jesus Christ of Nazareth, I command all evil alter speaking failure and evil into my life, to be burned down by the fire of God.

131. Horror and fear shall overwhelm the wicked, as You Lord face them with the greatness of Your power, all my enemies shall be afraid to move, they shall fall as silent as a stone, until I have passed through all danger to the blessings and preservation of God.

132. In this season, I will not fight to take what is rightfully my, the arm of the Lord shall bring me victory, the right hand of God shall fight my battle, in the name of Jesus. Father God let the light of Your face shine on me, for You love me.

133. Father with Your arm, break evil curses, vexes, hexes, jinxes, psychic powers, bewitchments, potions, charms, incantations, spells, witchcraft and sorcery, operating in my life and family, in the name of Jesus.

134. Pray that the arm of the Lord will come against unholy spirits, fallen angels, demons, empire of evil, and the entire Kingdom of Satan. Lord Jesus, rebuke in my life and my loved ones, councils, principalities, powers, world rulers, and wicked spirits in heavenly places, that are against us. I come against witches and wizards, chiefs and kings, princes, kingdoms, dominions, generals, rulers, captains, centurions, strongmen, and imps, in Jesus name.

135. Father God, preserve me from all evil, by Your great mercy, preserve my soul, thank You for preserving my going out and coming in, for all the days of my life, I shall be preserved by the Lord. Almighty God preserve me from financial problems, Father set me free from constant financial trouble, every

problem that money has brought into my life end, in the name of Jesus.

136. I command every frustration in my life to end today by the great power of God, financial frustration I cancel you, by the blood of Jesus, relational frustration and pain, come to a halt in my life, I reject physical frustration no more discomfort in my body or any areas of life.

137. Father heal all areas of my life, heal all family issues, career issues, heal emotional issues, Lord you know where I need healing more than I do, thank you for divine healing and restoration, in Jesus name.

138. Almighty God, be unto me a wall of fire that the enemy cannot touch, let the fire of God, protect me from every forces of darkness, protect our family from evil arrows, Lord be a wall of fire round about the body of Christ, in the mighty name of Jesus.

139. Father be a wall of fire to deliver us from financial devourer, do not permit the thief to steal from me any longer, in the name of Jesus. Lord, open new doors of financial breakthroughs for us, in the name of Jesus.

140. Father God, let Your glory be within us, let it abide with us, may Your glory rest upon all that we do, let it rest upon our homes, family, and ministry, in the name of Jesus.

141. Today, by the great power of God, I raise up a shout that will bless The Lord, a praise that will release my breakthrough,

worship that glorify God, and a shout that will bring down every Jericho wall and hindering my life, in the name of Jesus.

142. Pray say Almighty God, let my life show forth the marvelous work of God, when people see me, let them give glory to God, let my life bring praise to God, let all that know me thank God for my life, in the name of Jesus.

143. Anything standing in my life as a blemish, I command you in the name of Jesus vanish now Amen. Lord let all areas of blemish be removed, in the name of Jesus.

144. Almighty God, hold not Your peace, fight against those who fight against me, contend with those who contend with me.

145. I welcome all the ministry of the Holy Spirit in my life, in Jesus name.

146. Father Lord anoint me to start attracting good things into my life, anointing that will attract favor, goodness, blessings, and wholeness, come, in Jesus name.

147. Father God, I will look unto You, for everything that concerns me, I will look unto You for You alone are my hope, and helper, I will wait for The God of my salvation, I will wait for You Lord as long as I live, You are worth waiting for. Father may You hear me when I call, in the name of Jesus.

148. Lord do not let the wicked rejoice over me or any of my loved ones, in the name of Jesus. When I fall, I shall arise when I sit in darkness the LORD shall be a light unto me, let the glory light of God remove all darkness, and shine brightly over my life, in the name of Jesus.

149. Yoke of non-achievement, sickness, poverty, break, let every yoke of family bondage break in the name of Jesus. By the anointing of Almighty God, I have dominion over every satanic challenge in my life, marriage, finances, and ministry, I have dominion, by the power and authority of Jesus.

150. By the power of the blood of Jesus, the terror of the night shall not destroy my calling, my destiny, my children, or their calling. The terror of the night shall not swallow us up. For Jesus Christ of Nazareth, is Lord!!!

ABOUT THE AUTHOR: DR. PAT AKINDUDE

Dr. Pat is the President of Empowering Ministry Outreach and Lunch Date with Jesus Prayer Line in Houston, Texas. She has dedicated her life to empower others to be all they have been created to be, through her prayer, teaching, and counseling. She is a national and international speaker. She leads Prayer fellowship every last Friday of the month at 6300 Westpark Drive, Suite 310 in Houston. She is the author of the book, *Prayers That Get Answers* which focuses on praying effectively with scriptures. She also has prayer CDs that the Lord is using greatly.

As a former Director of Intercessory Prayer at Lakewood Church, Houston, Texas (from 2002 to 2014), she trained prayer partners for Lakewood Church and TBN. She is also the Author of 'Empowering Life Skills for Success', a customized training curriculum for nonprofit organizations. Her curriculum is used to train clients in transitional living and is being used in churches, schools, government agencies and nonprofit organizations. Organizations in Houston include Harris County adult education, Lakewood Church, Salvation Army, Red Cross, AID's Foundation, and Sally's House. Dr. Pat is dedicated to changing the patterns that hold people in bondage, by empowering them to break free from the cultural, mental, and physical limitations caused by wrong belief systems.

Dr. Pat Akindude: A spiritual leader, wife, author and a mother three beautiful children.

Education:

Bachelors in Business Administration

Masters in Counseling

PhD in Theology/Public Speaking

www.ingramcontent.com/pod-product-compliance
Lightning Source LLC
Chambersburg PA
CBHW032118090426
42743CB00007B/384